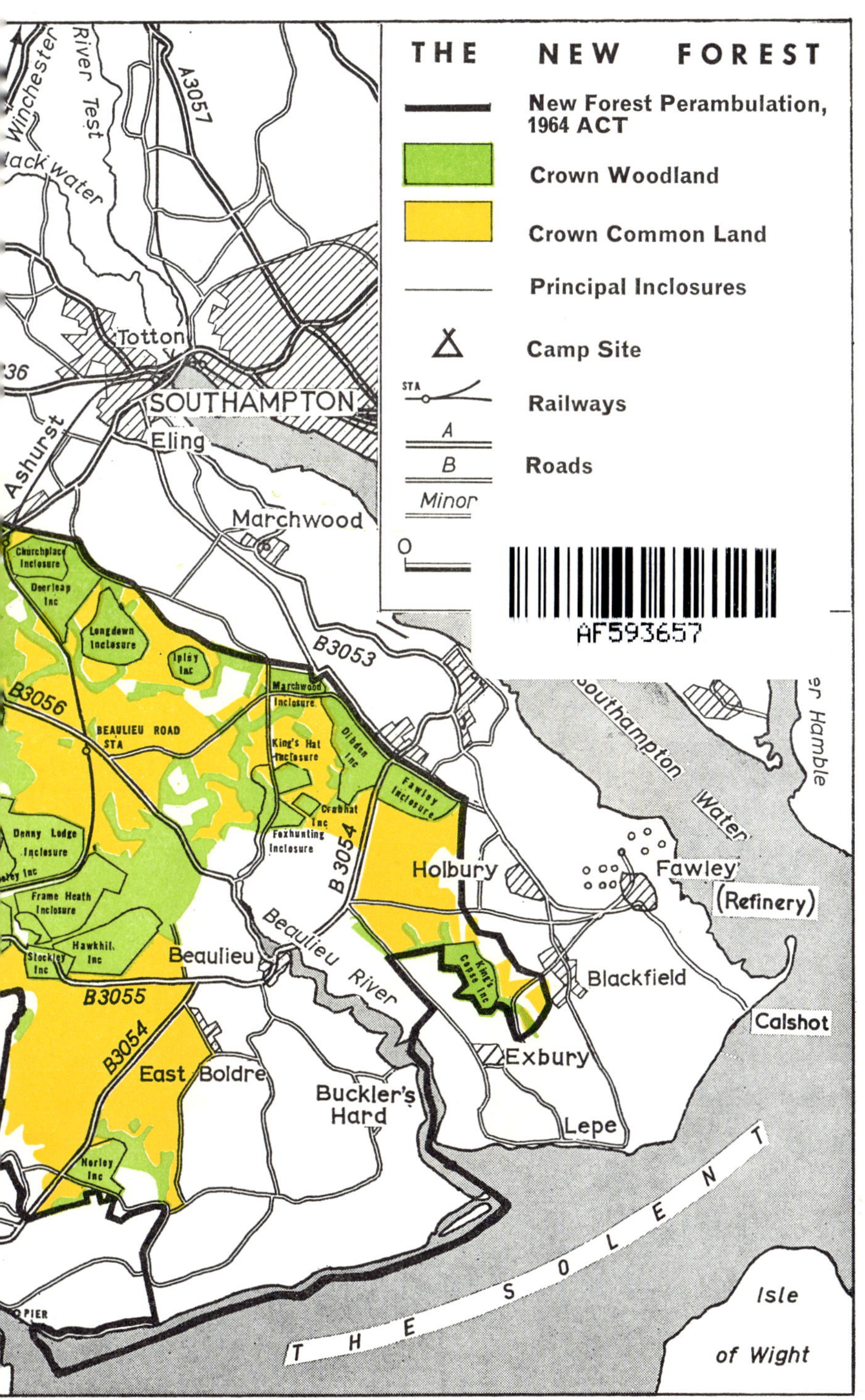
THE NEW FOREST
New Forest Perambulation, 1964 ACT
Crown Woodland
Crown Common Land
Principal Inclosures
Camp Site
Railways
Roads
A
B
Minor
STA
AF593657
Winchester
River Test
A3057
Totton
SOUTHAMPTON
Eling
Ashurst
Marchwood
Churchplace Inclosure
Deerleap Inc
Longdown Inclosure
Ipley Inc
B3053
B3056
BEAULIEU ROAD STA
Marchwood Inclosure
King's Hat Inclosure
Dibden Inc
Fawley Inclosure
Crabhat Inc
Foxhunting Inclosure
B 3054
Denny Lodge Inclosure
Frame Heath Inclosure
Hawkhill Inc
Stockley Inc
Beaulieu
B3055
B3054
East Boldre
Beaulieu River
Holbury
Fawley
(Refinery)
Southampton Water
Blackfield
Calshot
Exbury
Lepe
Buckler's Hard
Norley Inc
PIER
THE SOLENT
Isle of Wight

first published 1951
fourth edition 1969
Second impression (with amendments) 1973

NEW FOREST

The Open Forest

FORESTRY COMMISSION GUIDE

NEW FOREST

Foreword by
THE SEVENTH EARL OF RADNOR,
K.G., K.C.V.O.
Chairman of the Forestry Commission 1952–63

Edited by
H. L. EDLIN, B.Sc., Dip. For.
Forestry Commission

LONDON
HER MAJESTY'S STATIONERY OFFICE
1969

ACKNOWLEDGMENTS

THE COVER DESIGN and the pictures on pages 1, 22, 49–59, 63, 84, 86 and 97 are by C. F. Tunnicliffe, R.A. THE FRONTISPIECE and the picture on page 33 are by George Mackley, while Norman Wilson drew the Queen's House on page 15. Colin Gibson drew the picture on the sub-title page and also those on pages 3, 32, 47, 62 and 83. The drawings on pages 4 and 42 are by Ian T. Morison, D.A.

THE PHOTOGRAPHS. Thanks are due to the following photographers:

Mrs. T. K. Evans, of the Forestry Commission photographic staff, for the four pictures following page viii, and also for the four following page 92.

Following page 16: Maurice Nimmo, Douglas firs; Mr. W. J. Day, by courtesy of Miss Phyllis Holder, woodman; Mr. J. Tarlton, mares and foals and Open Forest; Forestry Commission, Knightwood oak.

Following page 32: Sport and General Press, Lymington River; Forestry Commission, fire tower; J. D. U. Ward, pigs; *The Times*, Bolton's Bench; T. M. Oldham, Scots pines.

Following page 48: Southern Newspapers, Lyndhurst and Beaulieu; J. H. Smith, Corsican pines; W. J. Day, Brockenhurst Church; J. Tarlton, Verderers Hall.

Following page 64: Roy Harris, fallow deer and ponies; Southern Newspapers, Brockenhurst; T. A. Wilkie, rounding up ponies; J. H. Smith, Corsican pines; Dr. J. K. St. Joseph, University of Cambridge, Mark Ash.

Following page 80: J. Tarlton, roe deer fawn, Queen's House, and pollard beeches; Roy Harris, lizard; Col. R. H. Palmer, grey squirrel; Geoffrey Kinns, fox cubs.

THE MAPS are based on the Ordnance Survey, by permission of the Director General, and have been prepared by Mr. W. J. Kennedy and Mr. Marc Sale.

THE POEM on page 84, by Thomas Hardy, is quoted by permission of Messrs. Macmillans; that on page 10, by Laurence Housman, is quoted by permission of Messrs. Jonathan Cape.

The article entitled "Motoring Without Maps in the New Forest", by Peter and Patricia Lewis, is included by kind permission of the magazine *Woman and Home*.

FOREWORD

by The Seventh Earl of Radnor, K.G., K.C.V.O.
Chairman of the Forestry Commission 1952–63

It has been my privilege for many years to be associated with the administration of the historic New Forest, which lies close to my own home in Wiltshire. The Forestry Commissioners have always kept in mind the manifold interests of those who share in its life, for the Forest is at once a great national reserve of timber, a grazing ground for several thousand cattle and ponies owned by the Commoners, and a region for recreation and the enjoyment of scenery and wild life, which, being open to the public at large, has much of the character of a National Park.

The New Forest, which has been a Crown possession since the days of the Normans, first came under the care of the Forestry Commission in 1924. In the year 1949, one of several New Forest Acts made provision for improvements in its management and revised the constitution of the ancient Court of Verderers, whose duties include the control of the Commoners' animals. Under this Act, the Commission has been empowered to make temporary enclosures in some of the Ancient and Ornamental Woods, with the object of restoring them as the old veteran trees decline and disappear.

In 1959, there was a further development under powers granted by the same Act. By agreement with the Verderers, 2,000 acres of open forest land was enclosed to provide fresh plantations, and also grazing strips for the cattle and ponies. The new woods have been sited along main roads, where their fences will check animals from straying on to the highway. Other recent changes have been the addition to the forest of certain charming woodlands on the Minstead Manor estate and the revision of the Perambulation under the New Forest Act, 1964.

For the full appreciation of the Forest it is necessary for the visitor to gain a closer knowledge of its topography, its wild life, and its long human history, than can be acquired merely by a drive or a ramble through its beautiful countryside. The editor of this Guide has been fortunate in bringing together a group of contributors who know the Forest intimately and from long experience. Its history, geology, flora and fauna are each described by an expert, while chapters on the woodlands have been contributed by a former

Deputy Surveyor of the Forest, the late Mr. D. W. Young, who had charge of them for many years, and by Mr. W. A. Cadman, another former Deputy Surveyor.

The freedom given to the public to enjoy the one hundred square miles of the New Forest in the Commissioners' charge, carries with it the obligation to observe the byelaws and to act in the spirit of the Country Code. The visitor must remember that the Forest provides a substantial share of the livelihood of the small farmers of the district, and gives employment to the large body of local men who tend its trees and harvest its timber. Both these activities can be gravely endangered by thoughtlessness with matches, tobacco or camp fires, which can all too easily result in a blaze raging over the heaths to blacken and destroy green and thriving woodlands, impoverish productive pastures, and spoil the scene for those who come after. Litter baskets have been provided at the more frequented spots, for the convenience of visitors, so that glass bottles and paper can be tidily disposed of, and not left as eyesores in the sylvan scene.

Two further points: to avoid the risk of accidents involving cattle or ponies, which have become all too frequent of late years, motorists are asked to exercise every care on the Forest roads; and picnic parties are asked to keep clear of ponds and streams in hot weather, as animals suffer distress if they cannot reach their watering places.

To all who will appreciate this unique expanse of tall forest and open heathland, it is my pleasant duty to extend, on behalf of the Forestry Commissioners, a cordial welcome to the enjoyment of its beautiful landscapes.

CONTENTS

continues overleaf

A young arboretum near Rhinefield, amid tall oaks and sprucewoods

B

Burning brushwood to clear planting ground in an Ancient and Ornamental wood

Quelling a gorse fire on the open heath

Foresters examining tall Douglas firs for seed crops, near the Ornamental Drive, Rhinefield

Tawny Owl

INTRODUCTION

THE New Forest, one of the largest areas of unenclosed land remaining in the south of Britain, has been aptly described as "a miraculous survival of pre-Norman England". It lies in the south-west of Hampshire, touching the shores of the Solent, and of the total area of 145 square miles within the perambulation, or legal forest boundary, no less than 105 square miles remain under public ownership; nearly all this Crown land, as it is called, is available for the access and enjoyment of the public. By the gradual processes of history, what was once the strictly preserved hunting ground of a despotic foreign conqueror has become the free heritage of every Englishman, and the purpose of this guide is to make its attractions better known to all.

The Forestry Commission, which administers this unique area, is the direct successor of the Lord Wardens appointed by the mediaeval kings to preserve their personal domain; and its principal officer in the Forest is still known by the ancient title of Deputy Surveyor. All the Royal Forests were formerly under the supervision of the Surveyor General, who was directly responsible to the monarch. The post of Surveyor General is no longer retained, but that of Deputy Surveyor, his deputy for a major forest, is still in use.

But it is timber production, rather than the hunting of the deer, that is now the main concern of the Crown, although its activities extend to the protection of wild life and the safeguarding of public amenities. The New Forest Commoners, descendants of men who pastured cattle and ponies on the Forest in Saxon times, still exercise their grazing rights; and disputes affecting these rights are still decided by the ancient Verderers' Court of Swainmote and Attachment, almost the sole survivor of the many powerful courts of Forest Law that once held sway over much of England, with powers of life and death over those who stole the King's deer.

Yet although the value of the Forest land for timber growing and stock raising has remained, and has even been increased by modern methods of forestry and agriculture, it has also acquired a new importance as an area for recreation.

Less than two hours from London by rail, and lying at the doors of the great seaport of Southampton and the populous seaside resort of Bournemouth, the New Forest still maintains much of its ancient detachment and freedom from the changes of present day civilisation. The broad high roads, by which the motorist or cyclist may reach it so easily from any part of the country, carry constant streams of traffic across it. But if one leaves the highways to turn aside into the wilderness of wood and moor, where oaks and beeches that number their years by centuries stand beside heaths that the plough has never broken, one returns almost at once to a primeval England. There are glades, moors, and marshes, deep within the Forest, that have scarcely changed since William the Conqueror decreed, in A.D. 1079, that this region should henceforth be his royal domain, so giving rise to the name of "New Forest" which it has held ever since.

The character of some of the original Forest, however, has changed during the succeeding 890 years. The Manors of Lyndhurst, Brockenhurst and Burley, which were in private hands when the Forest was made, and Beaulieu which was granted to the Church in 1204, have, with the relaxation of the old Forest Laws, been enclosed and partially built over; and other small areas have been lost by encroachment. Indeed, here and there the curious outline of some Forest homestead, jutting out into the surrounding waste land, shows that it was originally an "encroachment", built on land taken illegally from the open forest. But today, when the Forest is more jealously guarded, we can almost rank such losses as gains. For the villages and farmsteads are the strongholds of the Commoners, whose cattle, ponies, donkeys, pigs and geese add a picturesque element. By their grazing over the years, they have moulded the forest landscape, keeping its green lawns free from encroaching trees. Nor has the Forest been harmed by the later enclosures for timber growing, most of which were made in the nineteenth century, though some are far older. For this is now a long-established forest, in which trees of many different kinds and ages occupy relatively small stretches of ground, and where much regeneration of felled crops has been achieved by natural seeding of selected "mother trees". Although the Forest yielded no less than eight million cubic feet of timber during the 1914–18 war, and a further twelve-and-a-half million cubic feet during the 1939–45 war, these fellings were made with so careful an eye to the appearance of the woods, and re-growth since then has been so rapid, that the sylvan beauty of the plantations seems almost unimpaired.

Thus it is that the New Forest holds attractions for everyone: the historian searching for evidence of prehistoric or Roman occupation or wishing to visualise the land as the Normans knew it; the naturalist on the look-out for those rare birds, animals, or insects in which the Forest still abounds; the forester who wishes to study either natural or long-established planted woodlands; or the host of holiday makers who only seek some great expanse of pleasant open country over which they may wander at will. In the short chapters of this guide the authors, though each an expert on his subject and for long familiar with the ground, can only point the way to the fullest enjoyment of these pleasures. If you would learn more, the way lies open for you to delve more deeply into the Forest lore and to make your own explorations into this, the finest forest in all England.

Fox

The Rufus Stone

The Boast of Heraldry, the Pomp of Power

Gray

THE NEW FOREST IN HISTORY

BY MRS. M. GERARD DAVIS

A forest, it has been well said, *is* history. "There are forests in England where leafy noises may be shaped into Agincourt and the names of the battlefields of the Roses", wrote A. S. Smith in his *Dreamthorpe*, "oaks that dropped their acorns in the year that Henry VIII held his Field of Cloth of Gold, and beeches that gave shelter to the deer when Shakespeare was a boy". The oldest of the great English forests, so strangely now called *New*, is second to none in its power to quicken the imagination and conjure up the sense of the past. Since remotest antiquity its history has been linked to men's own. *Ytene*, "land of the Jutes", was inhabited long before the arrival of Norman kings. Here dwelt the dark Iberians of Neolithic times, that mysterious non-Aryan people who occupied France and Spain as well as the British Isles. After them came the tall, fair Goidels of the Bronze Age, who probably built Stonehenge and Sarum, and who brought the earlier inhabitants of this island into contact with the ancient civilisations of the Mediterranean world. Their circular burial mounds, still in many cases unexplored, are scattered through the heaths of the Forest. Then, as the Bronze Age faded into the Iron Age (it is a saddening thought that man records his history through his weapons), there came to the Forest that other Celtic people, the Britons, who have left their name to these islands, and whose civilisation continued to flourish in the Forest even after the Roman occupation.

Though the names of the towns like Winchester (*Venta Belgarum*) and Silchester (*Calleva Atrebatum*) bear testimony to the coming of the Romans to Hampshire, and although they had a town called *Clausentum* as near as Bitterne on Southampton Water, they settled but little within the Forest, whose waste spaces could hold but scant interest for them. But traces of a Roman village have been found on the forest fringes close to Nursling on the river Test, and just west of this, at Bossington, there was once unearthed a pig of lead weighing 156 pounds, inscribed as the property of the Emperor Nero, *consul* and *pontifex maximus*. The Romans occupied the camp of Buckland Rings, just north of Lymington, where coins of the Emperor Claudius have been found; and they also established potteries.

The most interesting traces of this period in the Forest are the remains of a flourishing pottery industry which have been discovered at various points in the north and west of the forest. Large mounds in this area were found to contain kilns and the remains of pottery of two kinds, a slate-coloured ware patterned with rough representations of leaves and grasses, and flat plates and dishes patterned in red and brown on a whitish ground, beautiful in themselves and particularly interesting as being amongst the few examples which have come down to us of British art in this period.

The main body of Teutonic settlers in the New Forest appears, from archaeological evidence, to have been the Jutes, who also settled in Kent, the Isle of Wight, and the Hamble district of Hampshire. But according to the *Anglo-Saxon Chronicle* the district was also the scene of the main invasion of the West Saxons, who landed in A.D. 495 at a place called "Cerdices ora", which has been variously identified as Hamble, Calshot, or Totton. Under their leaders Cerdic and Cynric, they defeated the British at "Natanleay" (possibly Netley Marsh) and advanced to "Cerdices ford", the modern Charford. They and their successors extended their conquests to form the kingdom of Wessex, with its capital at Winchester, which under Alfred the Great assumed the leadership of all England.

It was not until about the year 635 that Christianity came to Saxon Hampshire, and the place-names of the forest country show interesting traces of Old English heathenism—so Wheely Farm, a compound of the Old English *weoh* "heathen temple", and *leah* the Old English suffix meaning "a clearing in the wood". Or further to the north Froyle, from the Old English *Freohyll*, "the hill of the goddess Frig".

But it is with the Normans that most of us associate the Forest. And first and foremost with the policy of the Conqueror who, we once learned in childhood, laid waste a whole flourishing district of Hampshire to make himself a royal hunting ground, sacking villages, ruining homesteads and destroying churches with unexampled ruthlessness. And though in youth the gangster in us all may have tingled to this tale of spoliation, later judgment compelled us, sadly perhaps, to write the Conqueror on our list of "Bad Kings". Happily, such condemnation has been proved unnecessary. More recent scholarship has proved that the graver charges cannot be substantiated. The very nature of this furzy waste makes it (as Cobbett saw) impossible that the forestry country could ever have been a populous agricultural district. Moreover, the evidence of *Domesday* is conclusive. Here the account of holdings in William's reign, and in that of his predecessor Edward the Confessor, shows that although a certain amount of private property was requisitioned the district was by no means devastated; woodland and heath remained as before, sparsely interspersed with farms and homesteads.

Whence then the story? There seems little doubt that it represents an early and by no means unsuccessful piece of political propaganda; it is noteworthy that the policy of ruthless devastation is only attributed to King William much later than his own lifetime, when the misrule of his successors had made it very much to the interests of powerful persons and parties to discredit the ruling house. It is true, too, that there was in fact a serious grievance quite sufficient to vent itself in tales of ruthless spoliation; a grievance which sprang from the placing by William of the whole district under the hated Forest Law, with all that that involved of curtailment of liberty, and drastic punishment meted out for any infringement of its decrees, which were hurtful alike to every resident in the Forest, be he farmer or hunter. The idea of a forest specially preserved for royal hunting was not in itself new. Canute had imposed heavy fines on those who hunted in his forests, and Edward the Confessor had employed forest wardens, but never before had it been decreed that a man should be subject to maiming and death for the breaking of the forest laws. Thus it came about that when the Conqueror's son, Red William, was killed in Canterton glen on August 2nd, A.D. 1100, there were many to see in his untimely end a retribution for his father's efforts to subjugate the Forest. Twice already the Forest had taken toll of the Conqueror's family. One of his younger sons, Richard, had been gored to death by a stag. There is a record in *Domesday Book* of confiscated lands restored by William to their rightful owner as an offering for Richard's soul. A little later another Richard, illegitimate son of Duke Robert and nephew of William, had been killed when his horse dashed him against a tree.

Over the death of William Rufus there hangs a thick curtain of mystery. Every schoolchild learns, or used to learn, that the king was killed by an arrow shot by Sir Walter Tyrell, which glanced off an oak and struck him to the heart, as the inscription reproduced on page 9 relates. But debate still rages as to whether it was murder or merely death by misadventure:

> "I know not who the bow string drew,
> I know not how the arrow fled,
> Who bore the bow, the King who slew,
> I know not but t'was soothly said
> That Tyrell drew and the King lay dead."

In *The Killing of William Rufus* (1968), Duncan Grinnel-Milne presents a well-reasoned argument that Rufus was deliberately murdered by his younger brother Henry, who was ambitious for the throne. The deadly arrow was fired on Henry's orders by a huntsman, and Tyrell, a visitor from Normandy, was simply a convenient scapegoat who was made to take the blame. A most suspicious circumstance is that whilst Tyrell fled to Poole and thence to Normandy, Henry rode at once to Winchester to seize the national treasury. He then hastened to London where he persuaded the Bishop to anoint and consecrate him as king. All this was urgent because there was another heir with a better claim to the throne—Robert of Normandy who was older than both his brothers, William Rufus and Henry. From the speed at which all this was done, the author argues, the deed must surely have been premeditated.

William had plenty of enemies: the English whom he had oppressed, the churchmen whom he had robbed and insulted, the nobles whose allegiance he had exploited. And it is curious that many of these seem to have been expecting his untimely end. The details we shall probably never know. But for the forester the Red King still rides in the haunted glades. Ocknell Pond still runs red where Tyrell the regicide stooped to wash his hands as he started off on his long journey to Normandy. The story is still told of the smithy where Tyrell paused to have his horse re-shod, and which was sentenced for this to pay a fine in perpetuity to the Crown. Nor is Purkess the charcoal burner forgotten, who found the King's abandoned body and carried it on his cart to Winchester where "no bell was tolled, no prayer was said .... for the one baptised and anointed ruler whose eternal damnation was taken for granted by all men."

But the history of the Forest is not all as sinister and doom-laden as the story of Red William. The Cistercian abbey of Beaulieu, founded in 1204, was as gracious a flowering of human life as could be imagined. Yet if legend is to be believed, the roots of these good things go back to fear and greed and superstition. The story runs that King John, outraged by the hostility of the Cistercians, ordered certain of their abbots to be trampled to death by horses. His soldiers refused to carry out his behest and the abbots fled. Then the King in a dream saw himself hauled up before St. Peter for judgment and handed over to the abbots for a flogging, and woke up aching so much that to make amends he gave to the Order the magnificent site of Beaulieu. The Saxons long since had called it *beo-lea,* the bee meadow; the Normans called it *beau lieu,* the beautiful place. The buildings in their full splendour must have matched the site in beauty. The abbey church rose slowly, and to it were added the magnificent farm buildings, and the busy harbour served by ships from France and Spain and the Hanseatic towns. It was in this splendid setting that the monks of Beaulieu solved the problem of life by daily prayer to heaven and labour on earth. The monastery was dissolved in 1537, and passed into the hands of the Montagu family. But the ruined buildings still exist and something too of the ancient calm, something of a sanity which has gone from the world.

In the days of its prime the great abbey was often at the forefront of contemporary affairs. Pope Innocent III gave Beaulieu sanctuary rights, and so it came about that it was here that the unhappy Countess of Warwick fled when her husband Warwick "the King-maker" was slain at the Battle of Barnet in 1471. To Beaulieu, too, Perkin Warbeck the imposter fled when his troops had deserted him at Taunton. He left the shelter of Beaulieu only to become a prisoner at the Tower of London, and finally to pay at Tyburn the supreme penalty for his vaunting ambition.

And so through all the splendours and miseries of history the Forest played its part. So on November 13th, 1647, Charles I, outwitted and betrayed, fled through the Forest port of Lepe to Carisbrooke Castle on the Isle of Wight, to await the final act of the tragedy. So Monmouth in flight after Sedgemoor wrote his petition for mercy at Ringwood and, intending to seek refuge in the Forest until such time as he could take ship at Lymington for exile, was apprehended a few miles away from Ringwood at Woodlands Farm, crouching in a ditch overgrown with bramble by the tree which was henceforward known as Monmouth's Ash. Other fugitives of his rebellion sought shelter in the Forest, and it was for harbouring them that the gracious Dame Alice Lisle of Moyle's Court was sentenced to death by Judge Jeffreys in 1685.

While many probably know that the New Forest for long provided the bulk of the timber for our navy, it is perhaps less generally realized that in the eighteenth century the Forest possessed its own flourishing shipbuilding yards, and that the sleepy village of Buckler's Hard saw the construction of sloops, frigates and battleships, including ships as famous as Nelson's *Agamemnon*, which took part in his victories at Copenhagen and Trafalgar.

Those days are past. Gone, too, are the hard forest laws of an earlier period. But still the forest country has its own distinctive character, still it fulfils its traditional role of sanctuary, no longer perhaps for the political fugitive but for all who seek rest from the contemporary world with "its sick hurry, its divided aims," and who seek the bird-haunted quiet of its woodlands. "*Regum penetralia, et eorum maximae deliciae*—The secret retreat of kings, and chief of their delights."

INSCRIPTION ON THE RUFUS STONE

'Here stood the Oak Tree on which an arrow shot by Sir Walter Tyrrell at a Stag glanced and struck King William the Second surnamed Rufus on the breast of which he instantly died on the second day of August Anno 1100.

King William the Second surnamed Rufus being slain as before related was laid in a cart belonging to one Purkis and drawn from hence to Winchester, and buried in the Cathedral Church of that City.

That the spot where an Event so Memorable might not hereafter be forgotten the enclosed stone was set up by John Lord Delaware who had seen the Tree growing in this place.

This Stone having been much mutilated and the inscriptions on each of its three sides being defaced, this more Durable Memorial with the original inscription was erected in the year 1841 by William Sturges Bourne, Warden.'

Cloister Ruins, Beaulieu Abbey

How green the earth, how blue the sky
How pleasant all the days that pass
Here where the British settlers lie
Beneath their cloaks of grass!

LAURENCE HOUSMAN

ANTIQUITIES

BY H. L. EDLIN

IT cannot be said that the New Forest itself is rich in relics of the past, for settlers of bygone days avoided its sterile heaths and chose instead the fertile valleys and plains that surround it. Yet within a few miles of its borders lie several of the finest mediaeval buildings in the south of England, while the ruins of Beaulieu Abbey (illustrated above) show that fine architecture was once practised within the Forest itself.

PREHISTORY: BARROWS AND EARTHWORKS

Round barrows constructed by the prehistoric peoples of Britain are sufficiently numerous in the New Forest to add a characteristic touch to the moorland scene. Most of them stand upon slight eminences amongst the heaths, and a few are crowned by clumps of trees; Bolton's Bench, beside the Southampton road where it enters Lyndhurst village, is a familar example. Excavations into these tumuli have proved them to be burial mounds; most of those explored contained charcoal, funeral urns, and the remains of human bones, suggesting cremation of the dead, probably in Bronze Age times. No circles of standing stones have been discovered in the Forest, although Stonehenge, our finest example of such prehistoric structures, lies only fifteen miles to the north, at the heart of a region rich in remains of ancient occupation.

There are several defensive earthworks within the Forest which were probably first thrown up in prehistoric times. Several are known as "castles", but there is no clear evidence of mediaeval stone castles having been built in the Forest, though some of the mounds may have served as sites for wooden towers or "peles". The most conspicuous of these earthworks are Castle Hill on the west side of Godshill Inclosure (which commands a magnificent view across the Avon Valley to the Wiltshire Downs), another Castle Hill at Burley Street, and a long dyke which runs south-east from Bolton's Bench, Lyndhurst, and then swings south-west into Denny and Parkhill Inclosures. There are smaller mounds in Islands Thorns Inclosure (Studley Castle), Roe Wood, Sloden Inclosure, Churchplace Inclosure, and at Castle Malwood. The Bishop's Dyke, south of Beaulieu Road Station, is probably of prehistoric origin, though as it now encloses an impassable bog its original purpose is obscure. There is an amusing but ill-founded story that some jesting monarch gave the land it encloses to a certain Bishop of Winchester, who was allowed all the Forest ground he could crawl round—on his belly—in one day. Although no sensible bishop would have taken such a tortuous course or chosen such swampy soil, it is nevertheless true that the land within the ditch did belong to the church authorities, and only reverted to Crown ownership a few years ago.

RELICS OF THE ROMANS

In Roman times the New Forest was the centre of a thriving pottery industry, and numerous kilns have been discovered and excavated; several have been described and illustrated by the late Mr. Heywood Summer, F.S.A., in his *Excavations in New Forest Roman Pottery Sites*. The main pottery centre lies in and around what is now Sloden Inclosure; sites occur in Pitts Wood, Ashley Rails, Islands Thorns, and amongst enclosed fields north of Linwood, all in the north-east of the Forest. There is another group of kilns further south, in Anderwood and Oakley Inclosures to the east of Burley village. A typical kiln was about twelve feet in diameter and was constructed of puddled clay; it consisted of a combustion chamber, where wood or charcoal was burned with the aid of suitably arranged flues, and an upper dome wherein was arranged the pottery that was to be "fired". Many fragments of the actual pottery have been recovered, showing that this included a wide range of bowls, platters, flagons and mortars, decorated with incised or stamped designs. Coins found near the kilns suggest that they were worked until about A.D. 380.

There are two Roman roads in the Forest, but the connecting link between them has not been traced. The best known comes from Winchester; it follows the line of the present high road as far as Chandler's Ford, and then strikes across country through Chilworth to cross the Test by a Roman village site at Nursling, continuing through Copythorne to cross the present Forest boundary at Cadnam. From Cadnam to Stoney Cross its path coincides with the modern road to Ringwood, A.31. Beyond Stoney Cross it has been traced for a short distance north-east and south-west, suggesting a link-up with the two groups of pottery sites. The second Roman road lies in the extreme south-east of the Forest, and has been traced from Dibden Purlieu down to Lepe, a probable crossing place for the Isle of Wight. It is curious that few traces of Roman forts, villages, or villas have been discovered in the New Forest; but the Romans probably occupied the camp of Buckland Rings, near Lymington, and only a few miles away they had settlements at Bitterne (*Clausentum*), Winchester (*Venta Belgarum*), Old Sarum (*Sorbiodunum*) and Woodyates (*Vindogladia*).

Relics of Saxon days are too slight to call for mention, although the place-names of the Forest are, almost without exception, of Saxon or Jutish origin. The records of *Domesday Book* show that much of the land was uninhabited forest, and moorland, and after the coming of the Normans the retention of so much land as a royal hunting ground effectively prevented closer settlement. The few post-Norman buildings of interest to students of the past lie on the forest fringes, or else within its four enclaves of cultivated ground—Burley, Lyndhurst with Minstead, Brockenhurst, and Beaulieu. Nearly all are churches, for domestic buildings in the New Forest were built, until fairly recent times, of "cob", a form of puddled clay bound together with layers of heather; cob walls last well if kept thatched and dry, but most of these old buildings are now demolished and have left little trace; modern building is almost entirely in brick.

THE FOREST CHURCHES

For its size, the New Forest contains few parish churches of early date or great architectural interest. The reasons for this are the scarcity of good building stone, the sparse population and the fact that much of the forest serves as grazing grounds for parishes whose churches stand some distance beyond its boundaries, particularly on the north and west.

Although the tall, white spire of Lyndhurst church is an effective landmark that may be seen from far and wide across the Forest the building itself is a modern one of little interest to the antiquary; it contains, however, a wall painting by Lord Leighton, showing "The Ten Virgins". The little church at Emery Down is also a modern structure.

Minstead Church, some three miles north-west of Lyndhurst, has a stone chancel and nave erected in the thirteenth century, although the brick tower suggests a building of much later date. Peculiar interior features are a three-decker pulpit, a gallery, and two large private pews.

Brockenhurst Church is so old that it is mentioned in *Domesday Book*, and its dedication is unknown; most of the present building dates from the thirteenth century. Boldre Church includes work of twelfth century origin, though most of its structure is of somewhat later erection. The little churches at Dibden, Bramshaw, Fawley and Eling, are also of early date, having been built between the twelfth and fourteenth centuries. Those at Burley, Marchwood, Exbury and East Boldre are modern. There are notable old yew trees at Dibden, 30 feet round, and at Brockenhurst, 18 feet in girth.

ABBEYS, CATHEDRALS AND MINSTERS

Beaulieu Abbey is without doubt the finest mediaeval building within the Forest bounds, though only a fragment of its early splendour remains, and much of that is in ruins. It stands close to Beaulieu village, within a stone's throw of the peaceful tidal river Exe, or Beaulieu River, and the ecclesiastical buildings are open to visitors. The best preserved portion, still used as the parish church, was originally the monk's frater, one of the several out-buildings surrounding the central cloisters, the ruins of which are still to be seen. The original abbey church was a vastly greater structure, but of that only fragments remain. The Abbey was founded by King John in A.D. 1205 and was built of stone transported by water from Binstead in the Isle of Wight, Purbeck in Dorset, and Caen in Normandy, whilst the roofing slates were brought from Cornwall. It was a Cistercian foundation, and the monks farmed extensive lands reaching down to the Solent, which are still a fertile enclave within the New Forest heaths. They are said to have kept cattle at Beaufre (boeuf=bull), sheep at Bergerie (berger=shepherd), and fish in Sowley Pond; and they had a chapel and a grange at St. Leonards.

Not far beyond the Forest bounds lie Romsey Abbey and Christchurch Priory, magnificent churches rich in Norman work which proclaims their early foundation. Going a little further afield, one may reach Winchester Cathedral, the fine old Minster church of Wimborne, or Salisbury Cathedral with its splendid soaring spire. All these lie near enough to the Forest to have played their part in its history, and they may remind the visitor that, although the New Forest itself is poor in great churches, it lies at the hub of one of the richest and most early developed districts of England.

DOMESTIC ARCHITECTURE

As we have seen, the New Forest has always been a thinly-peopled area, poor in building stone, and these facts, together with the Crown ownership of so much of the land, effectively hindered the development of great castles or manor houses within its bounds. Many of the large country houses were built in Victorian days, when the Forest became fashionable as a residential area. At Lymington, however, the maritime trade of the eighteenth century led to the building of at least one fine street of Georgian houses, with an attractive church in Restoration style to match. Hythe, too, on Southampton Water, has about it an atmosphere of sailing ship days. At Buckler's Hard, near Beaulieu, one may see the slipway whence wooden men-of-war were launched into the Exe, with the houses of the old carpenters still standing on either side, a fit setting for its new maritime museum.

The Queen's House

Waken, lords and ladies gay,
To the greenwood haste away,
All the jolly chase is here
With hawk and horse and hunting-spear

SCOTT

THE QUEEN'S HOUSE, LYNDHURST

BY H. L. EDLIN

THE Queen's House is the principal building owned by the Crown within the historic New Forest, and is the centre of the Forest administration. It is called "The Queen's House" when a Queen is reigning, and "The King's House" when a King occupies the throne. The present structure is a large three-storey brick building dating mainly from the reign of Charles II, but altered and restored on several occasions since. It stands on a hilltop at the head of the Lyndhurst High Street, next to the parish church. There are records and some slight remains, of earlier buildings here.

To understand the history of this building and its predecessors, it is necessary to remember that they have served, at different times, four functions:—

1. The Manor House of the Royal Manor of Lyndhurst.
2. A Royal Residence.
3. A Court of Justice.
4. The Administrative Office of the New Forest.

But first a word about its site. Both the road plan and the levels of the land in Lyndhurst have been altered over the years, so we must visualise it as it was in the past. The tall church just east of the Queen's House stands on an artificial mound. Originally the Queen's

House occupied a prominent knoll with no higher ground to the north-east, east, south, or south-west; its elevation is 150 feet above sea level. This knoll was originally the meeting place of tracks from townships that have, by reason of their situations, a long history. Southampton, Beaulieu, Lymington and Christchurch (anciently Twynham) all stand at the head of inlets of the sea. Ringwood, Fordingbridge, Salisbury (anciently Sarum), Romsey and Winchester are all old settlements at river crossings.

Originally the New Forest comprised all the land between the River Avon on the west, Wiltshire on the north, the River Test and Southampton Water on the east, and the Solent to the south. This knoll, where so many tracks met, was close to its geographic centre. Therefore William the Conqueror chose the Manor of Lyndhurst, and probably this very hillock, as the centre of his Forest administration. Lyndhurst was the only Royal Manor within the Forest.

In earlier times, before the fields of Lyndhurst had been enclosed the forest tracks converged more directly on the Queen's House than the roads do now. A map dated 1811, and some early prints, show a road striking south-west from a point near the west end of the building; this probably led to Bank, across what is now Cuffnells Park, and so towards Christchurch. Other approach roads were closed in the nineteenth century. No neighbouring building is as old as the Queen's House.

I. THE ROYAL MANOR OF LYNDHURST

Historians now believe that the first Teutonic settlers in the New Forest were the Jutes, who arrived, probably from Jutland in Denmark, in the fifth century. The Saxons, who came to Wessex in strength in A.D. 495, called this region Ytene, meaning "the Jutes' country". The place name of Lyndhurst suggests an early settlement; it was spelt as "Linhest" in 1086 and "Lindeherst" in 1165. "Lynd" signifies lime tree, and the existence of lime as a wild tree in the Forest is confirmed by pollen deposits. "Hurst" originally meant a wooded hillock, and the frequency and distribution of "hurst" names for south-eastern villages suggests that such places were favoured for settlements made in very early times. Lyndhurst is thus "the village on the hillock of lime trees".

The recorded history of Lyndhurst begins about the year A.D. 980, when it was already a royal manor. The Saxon Queen Elfrida then gave it, or possibly the income from it, to the Abbey of Amesbury in Wiltshire. In the reign of Edward the Confessor (1044–1066) Lyndhurst Manor was taxed at £6 a year.

Douglas Firs, 140 feet tall, in Bolderwood Grounds

Woodman and apprentice, circa 1910, outside a Woodman's cottage built one hundred years earlier

Mares and foals on the windswept heath

Open forest grazing grounds near Rhinefield

The Knightwood Oak

The first Norman king, William I, who conquered England in 1066, created his "New" Forest over the land of Ytene about the year 1079. When his Domesday Book was compiled, in 1086, he had taken this manor back into his own hands. As part of the process of making his hunting ground, he "afforested", or threw back into the wastes, much of the cultivated land of the Forest Manors.

The only land taxed at Lyndhurst in 1086 was assessed as one virgate, held by Herbert the Forester, who was doubtless a Crown official; this was valued at only 10s. 0d. a year. But later records show that the manor became a useful agricultural property; it may have equalled in size the present enclosed lands around the village.

The actual Domesday entry runs as follows:—

"In Bovere Hundredo.

Ipse Rex tenet Linhest. Jacuit in Ambresberie de firma Regis. Tunc, se defendebat ii hidis. Modo, Herbertus forestarius ex his ii hidis unam virgatam (tenet), et pro tanto geldat, aliae sunt in foresta. Ibi modo, nichil, nisi ii bordarii. Valet x solidos. Tempore Regis Edwardi valuit vi libras."

This has been translated as follows:—

"In Bovere Hundred.

The King himself holds Linhest which appertained to Ambresberie (Amesbury) which is of the Kings ferm (a taxation unit). It was then assessed at 2 hides. Of these 2 hides, Herbert the Forester holds now 1 virgate, and pays geld for that amount; the remainder is in the forest. There are now only 2 bordars (cottagers). It is worth ten shillings. In the time of King Edward the Confessor it was worth six pounds."

(*Note.* 2 hides would be *about* 240 acres, and 1 virgate *about* 30 acres.)

Ever since the Conqueror's day this manor has remained in the hands of the Crown. The enjoyment of it has been granted on various terms to tenants of varying status, including Queens of England, noble dukes, landed gentry, and forest officials. Many, though not all, of these tenants were at the same time Lord Wardens of the New Forest, and thus responsible for its administration.

In 1299 there was a park "attached to the Manor of Lyndhurst", covering 500 acres. There is a reference in 1313 to "the close (enclosed lands) of Queen Margaret at Lyndhurst". Later in that century there is mention of "inclosing the King's Park at Lyndhurst", and timber was sold from this park in 1359. In 1359, "by the advice of the keeper of the forest", the Manor was enclosed with a ditch and a hedge, and there were further outlays on park fencing in 1387 and 1428. Old grants distinguished between the "Manor" and the "Park", but by the beginning of the 17th century, the "Old

Park of Lyndhurst" was described as arable land and woodland. All this points to the existence of a productive agricultural holding at Lyndhurst, from an early date, in contrast to the picture of devastation given by the Domesday Book. But it is not possible to trace the extent of the old park and manorial fields on the present-day map of Lyndhurst; much of the ground has passed to private ownership.

The last tenant of the Manor was Mr. George Harrison, who held it from 1827 to 1831. Since 1852 the Deputy Surveyors of the New Forest have been *ex officio* Stewards of the Manor of Lyndhurst. The last manorial court, or court baron, was held in 1895, and by 1903 only one copyhold property survived. Some of the old manorial lands are now held as freeholds by the Crown and a few Lyndhurst farms still hold the right of "estovers", entitling them to a free supply of wood for fuel and repairs, by virtue of having once formed part of the "homage" of the manor. Otherwise the manorial customs have lapsed.

It was customary for every manor to have a manor house as the home of its lord, or his steward or tenant. The Queen's House is, in its first origin, such a manor house. The first record of a building dates from about 1300, in the reign of Edward I, when an order was issued for "twenty oaks to make laths for the use of the Queen's manor house at Lyndhurst", apparently for the repair of an existing building. We know from this that a manor house has stood here for 660 years, at least.

Often a parish church is associated with a manor. Lyndhurst was probably a parish with its own rector until 1279. Thereafter, until 1928, it was regarded as a chapelry attached to the neighbouring Parish of Minstead. At least three churches have stood on the mound east of the church—an early English one, a Georgian one built in 1740, and the present Victorian Gothic one dated 1860. All the New Forest churches stand on mounds, either natural or artificial; that at Lyndhurst is clearly artificial.

2. THE ROYAL RESIDENCE

Whether a royal manor house was actually lived in by the sovereign depended largely on his personal inclinations. If he did reside in it, he might enlarge it to a size greater than the manor itself could support, by drawing on his other revenues, and this has happened at Lyndhurst. The attraction here has, of course, been the sport of hunting in the New Forest, and the trees of the Forest supplied the necessary capital.

The first Queen of Edward I, Eleanor of Castile, made Lyndhurst her home, during the absences of the King on his wars against the

Welsh, *circa* A.D. 1280. The second Queen of Edward I, Margaret of France, held the Manor of Lyndhurst from 1299 to 1318, during the Scottish wars. Queen Isabel, widow of Edward II, held it from 1318 to 1330, and Philippa, the Queen of Edward III, was in possession from 1330 to 1332.

During the reign of Henry VIII (1509 to 1547) the "old house" was repaired and enlarged. The old porch and the first storey of the east wall of the building, which is Tudor in design and is built of peculiar small bricks, date from this period.

The main rebuilding of the manor house as a royal abode was carried out between 1634 and 1672. It was begun by Charles I and completed, after the Civil War, by his son Charles II. The money was raised, in part at least, by the sale of timber, lops and tops, from the Forest. A warrant dated 1635 authorised the sale of 250 loads of timber "at the highest profit" for this purpose. The first estimate for the work was £1,563 12s. 6d., but it is clear that at least £2,000 was spent. In addition, much oak timber was drawn from the New Forest woods. The work was begun under letters patent from Charles I to John Chamberlayne of Lyndhurst, which called for:

> "the new building of divers lodgings for our use and service adjoyning to the old house at Lyndhurst in the Newe Forrest, as also, a Kitchyn, Pastrie, Larder and other offices, and a stable to contain fortie horse according to the plots and directions given by the Surveyours of our Workes".

The building so constructed consists of much of the present Queen's House to the west of the Verderers' Hall, but the stables, which stood on the far side of the main road, have vanished.

Contemporary records, as well as the size of the stables, make it clear that the purpose of the residential part of the present building was to serve as a royal hunting box. Charles I certainly hunted from Lyndhurst; and in all probability Charles II and James II did likewise. Thereafter the only sovereign to stay at the Queen's House was George III, who came here in 1789.

In the absence of the King, the Queen's House was used as a residence by one of the Forest Officials, at first the Lord Warden, but subsequently by the Deputy Surveyor.

In 1789 the Duke of Gloucester, in his capacity of Lord Warden of the New Forest, acted as host to George III. There were no further visits by the reigning sovereign, but the last three Lord Wardens, namely the Dukes of Gloucester, York, and Cambridge, were all members of the royal house. The last royal tenant was His Royal Highness Prince Adolphus Frederick (Hanover), Duke of Cambridge, the seventh son of George III; he held it from 1827 until his death in 1850.

From 1851 to 1915, the Queen's House was the official residence of the Deputy Surveyor of the New Forest, the occupants being Lawrence Henry Cumberbatch, 1851–1880, and the Honourable Gerald Lascelles, 1880–1915. Subsequently, the residential part of the building was leased to private occupiers. In 1965 the whole was converted to its present purpose of administrative offices for the Forest.

3. THE COURTS OF JUSTICE

The Forest Laws enacted by William the Conqueror and his successors required for their enforcement four kinds of courts of justice, each with its peculiar powers. These were the Court of the Chief Justice in Eyre, and the Courts of Regard, Swainmote, and Attachment. Their functions and importance have varied with the passing of time, and today the only survival, in a much altered form, is the "Court of Swainmote and Attachment", generally known as the Verderers' Court.

From the earliest days a hall in which the courts could meet was needed. Such a hall was built within or beside the old manor house, in 1388, and has since become known as the Verderers' Hall. The present structure is believed to occupy the same site as this one. Parts go back to Tudor days, as shown by the small bricks used for the porch, but the whole has been much altered by reconstructions.

The last Court of the Chief Justice in Eyre was held here in 1669, during the reign of Charles II. It was presided over by Vere, Earl of Oxford, and the hatchment of the Royal Arms, which was then displayed, is still preserved and on view.

Another relic is related to the ancient Court of Regard, which laid down what dogs might be kept within the forest. This is an iron stirrup, apparently of Tudor date, and it is said that any dog which could crawl through it was too small to require "expeditation". Expeditation originally meant cutting off a dog's claws so that it could not chase the deer; later on, the payment of a fine was substituted for the actual operation. But if the story about a stirrup is true, it is unlikely that the particular one displayed was so used; its pattern suggests too late a date of origin. It may, however, be related to the traditional (Lord Warden's) badge of office of the Forest administration, which is a stirrup surmounted by a crown.

The Hall also contains a very old prisoners dock, built of solid oak, hewn to shape with the adze, one particularly solid bench, and two old oak tables that may be of Tudor date. Otherwise the furniture and fittings are modern.

Today the hall is still used for the meetings of the Verderers' Courts, which are held every other month and are open to the public. Under the New Forest Acts, 1877 and 1949, the Official Verderer, who presides over the meetings, is appointed by the Queen under sign manual, to hold office during the royal pleasure. Certain of the other verderers are elected and certain of them are nominated. The Official Verderer and a select few of the others exercise judicial powers, and for this purpose they are specially nominated by the Lord Chancellor.

Except when required for official purposes, the Verderers' Hall is open, free of charge, to the public, between 9 a.m. and 5 p.m. on Mondays to Fridays inclusive.

4. AN ADMINISTRATIVE OFFICE

Originally the management of a Royal Forest was carried on by a number of officials, each with a picturesque title and a particular function to perform. The most important was the Lord Warden, and in the New Forest this office was usually, though not always, held by the tenant of the Royal Manor of Lyndhurst. This office eventually became a sinecure, and on the death of the last Lord Warden, His Royal Highness the Duke of Cambridge, in 1849, no further appointment was made.

The active management of the Forest was devolved, under a legal process in 1760, on a Surveyor-General of Woods, Forests, and Land Revenues of the Crown. This was an ancient office, first established by Henry VIII. The Surveyor-General's representative in the New Forest bore the title of Deputy Surveyor, and this title has been retained to the present day.

In 1810 Commissioners of Woods, Forests and Land Revenues were appointed to hold and administer the Royal Forest property. The management of the New Forest was thereafter carried out by a Commissioner of Woods, with his office in London, and a Deputy Surveyor stationed in or near Lyndhurst.

In 1850 it was decided to remove the Deputy Surveyor's office from New Park, near Brockenhurst, to the Queen's House, which is better placed for the Forest as a whole, and it has remained here ever since. At first only a small part of the building served this purpose, but now the whole structure has been restored and adapted for this use.

In 1924 the management of the New Forest was transferred to the Forestry Commission, a body corporate consisting of ten Commissioners, each appointed by the Queen, by warrant under the sign manual, for a stated term of years. The ancient link of the Forest's administration with the Crown is thus preserved. The present Chairman of the Forestry Commission is Lord Taylor of Gryfe.

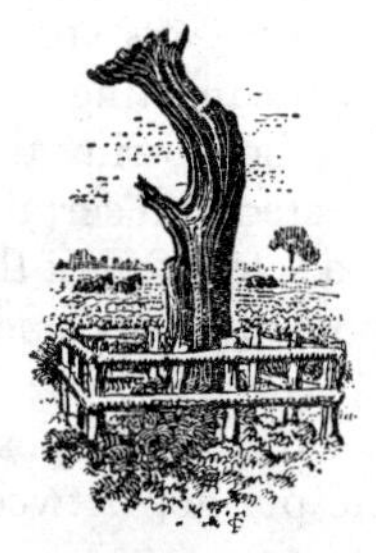

The Naked Man—
Sentinel of the Heaths

. . . In the stir of the forces
Whence issued the world.

MATTHEW ARNOLD

THE GEOLOGICAL STRUCTURE OF THE NEW FOREST

BY L. E. TAVENER

MUCH of Southern England consists of broad shallow basins, such as the London Basin and the Hampshire Basin, which are filled with gravels, sands and clays and are surrounded by low chalk downlands, such as the Chiltern Hills, the North Downs, and the Hampshire Downs. The New Forest lies in one of these shallow basins—the Hampshire Basin—and the form of the surface features, the nature of the soils, and the type of vegetation result to a marked extent from this fact.

We shall discover, as we begin to explore the Forest, that there are three main types of surface form; infertile, flat-topped, gravel plateaux or sandy plains; rich, well-drained clays and loams where somewhat older geological series are exposed; and broad areas of low-lying, ill-drained marshland. Closely associated with these land forms are three distinct types of natural vegetation:

Heathland—barren areas, with a few self-sown Scots pine and birch, gorse, heath, and various hardy grasses.

Woodland—either beech or oak, with yew, holly and thorn.

Marshland—with alder thickets, willows, heath, bracken, sedge, bog-moss and cotton grass.

First of all we shall notice many wide expanses of exposed, flat-topped plateaux or level plains. They have the appearance of infertile, barren heathlands, more like the Scottish moors than "forest", and they occur in widely separated parts of the New Forest. From Telegraph Post, along the Downton-Cadnam Road, where the plateaux reach their highest point—419 feet—the land slopes gently southward, and also south-westward towards the River Avon. This most northerly part of the Forest, lying between the Downton-Cadnam Road and the Ringwood-Cadnam Road, consists of a series of flat-topped, parallel ridges—Deadman Hill, Hampton Ridge, Ibsley Common and Hasley Inclosure, Broomy Walk, and Handy Cross. Each ridge is capped by about twelve to fourteen feet of broken, water-worn, chalk flints, interspersed with sand and small pebbles. Streams have cut deep valleys through the gravel cappings, and not only washed away much of the gravel that once formed a continuous spread over the whole area, but also exposed different and older strata as they have cut more deeply into the land surface. On Beaulieu Heath we shall come across a similar type of landscape, but here the plains are lowerl and wider; the texture of the surface soil is that of a sandy-gravel; and the rivers have not cut out deep valleys. These flat, gravelly pateaux and plains, usually treeless and covered with gorse and heather, can be noted in many other parts of the Forest and form a striking contrast to the more wooded areas.

The second feature is the somewhat scattered distribution of thick natural woodlands, usually of beech or oak, and containing much thorn, holly and yew. These woodland areas usually cover the long, gentle slopes that separate the flat-topped plateaux. In these areas, the soil consists of clay or sandy loam, with occasional beds of quartz and rounded pebbles. The clays are sometimes dark and greenish in colour; and in places there are bands or "beds" of yellow sand with layers of white pipe clay. If we are fortunate, we may find in these seams the remains of a few sub-tropical plants and marine fossils; such as corals, *Solenastrea granulata* Duncan, *Lobopsammia cariosa* Goldfuss, and other species; and many shells.

In Roman times pottery was made from these clays, and a number of Roman kilns have been discovered at Crook Hill, Panshard Hill, Sloden, Anderwood and Oakley Inclosures, Islands Thorns and other places. At Beaulieu, bricks were once made from the clays, and at Brockenhurst there were formerly kilns for making pottery, tiles, drain pipes, etc., as well as bricks.

The third characteristic feature is the abundance of broad, low-lying areas of ill-drained marshland, with a vegetation cover of alder thickets, heath, bracken, sedge, bog-moss and cotton grass. These areas occur, for the most part, in the lower parts of the Forest, and especially along the borders of the lower courses of the rivers where a greenish loam is deposited along the river bottoms in flood time.

In several places, as at Wilverley Walk and Matley Bog, conditions are found favouring the formation of peat. Water-logging, however, is not confined to the lower areas, and, surprisingly, much bog occurs on the plateau sections.

THE DEVELOPMENT OF THE LANDSCAPE

It is interesting to trace the development of these various changes in the landscape, and to find out why the Forest should lie in a comparatively low, shallow basin, surrounded by chalk downland; why extensive gravel-spreads cover much of the land-surface; what gave rise to the beds of fertile dark greenish clays; and why so much of the Forest is waterlogged and marshy.

At one time—during what geologists call the Cretaceous (Chalk) Period—the land where the New Forest now stands was covered to a great depth by an ocean which extended over much of Northern Europe. On the floor of this ocean the shells of microscopic marine creatures (*Foraminifera*) accumulated, and gradually became pressed together into a hard mass of chalk. In course of time the sea floor was raised very slowly and irregularly until part of the chalk beds was exposed above sea-level to encircle broad shallow troughs, many of which remained submerged beneath shallow seas. Soon large rivers began to drain the exposed land surfaces and to carry eroded material down to the shallow seas, where layers of earthy matter and pebbles and bits of dead vegetation accumulated. The deposits suggest that the Forest area may have been occupied by a large river estuary or shallow sea that extended across Western Europe as far as the Ardennes in Belgium. As soon as the rivers entered the sea, their speed was checked and the heaviest part of their load, such as pebbles, was dropped; farther out, the sands were deposited; and the clays and ooze were carried farthest from the shore.

Subsequently, earth movements raised these shallow basins above sea level, exposing the more recent—Eocene or Tertiary—deposits which had accumulated in them. Upon this surface the present form of the land surface began to take shape; a broad shallow basin —the Hampshire Basin—filled with Tertiary clays and sands and surrounded by a low rim of chalk downlands. The northern downland rim can be traced from Cranborne Chase through the Wiltshire and Hampshire Downs to the west, north and east of the Forest. The southern downland rim is represented by Ballard Down in the Isle of Purbeck and the central chalk ridge of the Isle of Wight, but much of it has been eroded away and lies below sea level. Erosive agencies started immediately to wear away these various exposed land surfaces, and to break down much of the flints of the chalk downlands into angular fragments.

It appears that the whole area was affected once more by some drift agency, possibly associated with the closing phases of the Glacial Period, which carried these gravels and other sandy material over the central parts of the basin to form the gravel spreads (Plateau Gravel and Valley Gravel) that cover much of the clays and sands (Tertiary) that had been previously deposited. As river action began to wear through these gravel cappings the older, more regular beds of clays and sands were exposed. For instance, in the area between the Downton-Cadnam Road and the Ringwood-Cadnam Road, the plateau-gravel ridges are separated by deeply cut valleys where streams have washed away much of the gravel cappings and exposed the older geological formations on which the gravels rest; in the north, Millersford Bottom and Ditchend Brook expose the Bagshot Sands; in the centre, Latchmore Bottom and Dockens Water expose, for the most part, the Bracklesham Beds; and in the south is Linford Water, along whose flanks the Barton Beds outcrop. A most interesting correlation of soil type and natural vegetation may be made by walking from one Plateau Gravel capping, across a valley, and up to the plateau on the other side. Two distinct types of landscape have developed as a result of these conditions; the barren, gravel-capped plateaux, and the more fertile, wooded slopes.

It now remains to explain the waterlogging that characterizes much of the Forest. As a general rule, the surface water percolates through the gravels and sands and is held up by the clay beds, which then direct the flow and usually determine where the springs appear at the surface. In some places the drainage is impeded before it reaches the clay; soluble minerals are washed down and accumulate to form a hard-pan or impermeable layer, at a depth of from one to three feet from the surface. Consequently, the surface soil becomes both impoverished and waterlogged; and this accounts for the poverty of many of the Forest soils; and also for the bog and marsh which occur even in those areas where sands or gravels form the surface cover. In some cases, where the drainage is particularly held up, shallow ponds are caused to form, such as Ocknell Pond and Janesmoor in the north, and Whitten in the south. The larger ponds in the Forest are few in number and of artificial origin. A rusty red can be detected, colouring most of the gravels, and the presence of iron and other minerals in the streams flowing through the gravels is supposed to have beneficial effects *e.g.* Iron's Well or Leper's Well in Eyeworth Walk.

Bog Gentian, Gladiolus, Cotton Grass, and Bog Asphodel

Thanks to the human heart by which we live,
Thanks to its tenderness, its joys, and fears,
To me the meanest flower that grows can give
Thoughts that too often lie too deep for tears.

WORDSWORTH

WILD FLOWERS IN THE NEW FOREST

BY MARY GOODHART

THE New Forest is a compact area of great interest botanically. It is surrounded on the north and west by the chalk downland of the Hampshire and Dorset downs, but it is quite without this type of land within its boundaries.

Roughly the Forest can be divided into two types of land which produce a striking difference in vegetation. First the Plateau Gravel which can be seen at its best, perhaps, from the Cadnam-Stoney Cross-Ringwood road and north-west from Stoney Cross to Godshill. Parts of this high land are well over 400 feet, and its drops steeply on the western edge of the Avon valley, and much more gradually to the south and east. This type of heathland also extends to the east at a rather lower level from Lyndhurst to Beaulieu Heath. The rest of the Forest is roughly made up of clays and loams, some well drained and some forming large areas of bog land.

These two areas are far the most interesting botanically and it is here that one finds old mixed woods, streams, bogs and ponds. The different types of flora that we can consider are heathlands, woods, bogs and sea shore.

HEATH

Let us now look in more detail at the high open heathlands. Large areas of this are covered with two heathers—the bell heather (*Erica Cinerea*) with its vivid purple spikes of bell-shaped flowers which flower from early summer, and later in the year the ling (*Calluna vulgaris*) of a much paler mauve. These two cover great stretches of these high lands. A third heath—the crossed leaf (*Erica tetralix*) is also found in the damper parts, but this is more frequent in the boggy parts of the Forest, rather than on the uplands. In amongst the heather there is a good deal of dwarf gorse (*Ulex minor*) which is low growing and not quite so prickly as the common gorse (*Ulex europaeus*) which makes a glorious blaze of colour in the spring, and is very widespread. One other gorse (*Ulex gallii*) is also to be found here and there, as well as the pretty little petty whin (*Genista anglica*).

The spotted orchis (*Orchis ericetorum*) flourishes on these heathlands too, usually in a rather stunted form. Bracken (*Pteridium aquilinum*) of course crops up everywhere both on the high and low lands and makes a blaze of colour in the autumn adding greatly to the beauty of these otherwise rather bleak highlands. There are other small flowers growing amongst the heather such as milkwort (*Polygala serpyllifolia*), cinquefoil (*Potentilla reptans*) and tormentil (*P. erecta*).

Of trees there are few, but here and there stand a few self-sown Scots pine, birch and thorn.

We can now turn to the loams and clays which make up the rest of the New Forest. These lie at a lower level than the Plateau Gravel and are much more varied and fertile. In this area we find the extensive decidous woods which are one of the chief beauties of the Forest both in the spring and autumn. The streams and bogs and ponds also lie in this area.

WOODS

These natural woods are made up chiefly of beech, oak, holly and blackthorn, and where they are fairly open, a great number of flowers flourish from earliest spring till late summer. Among the very early woodland flowers to be found is the spurge laurel (*Daphne laureola*) in a few places, soon followed by wood spurge (*Euphorbia amygdaloides*) which is abundant in all parts, primroses (*Primula vulgaris*) in selected spots, wood anemone (*Anemone memorosa*), wood sorrel (*Oxalis acetosella*), bluebells (*Endymion nonscriptus*) and in some areas daffodils (*Narcissus pseudo-narcissus*) still flourish. In a few places can be found the golden saxifrage (*Chrysosplenium oppositifolium*), while even lily of the valley (*Convallaria majalis*) can still be found in small quantities. The orchid family is well represented too. The early purple orchis (*Orchis mascula*) often grows amongst the bluebells, the two butterfly orchids (*Platanthera bifolia* and *P. chlorantha*), birds nest (*Neottia nidus-avis*), twayblade (*Listera ovata*), broad and marsh helleborine (*Epipactis helleborine* and *E. palustris*) and the green winged orchid (*Orchis morio*) are all to be found.

In a few damp woods the yellow balsam (*Impatiens noli-tangere*) is happily on the increase. The butchers broom (*Ruscus aculeatus*) flourishes in several areas in spite of being picked now extensively for Christmas decorations instead of, as in the olden days, by butchers to make bunches of it with which to clean their chopping blocks. The columbine (*Aquilegia vulgaris*) still holds its own on the edges of some woods and down the rides, as does also the rather spectacular bastard balm (*Melittis melissophylum*), with its conspicuous white and reddish-purple flowers, which reaches a height of two to three feet in favourable conditions. The lungwort (*Pulmonaria longifolia*), which here has one of its strongholds in the country, is to be found sometimes in woods and sometimes on banks in the open. Other plants to be found growing equally happily in or out of the woods are yellow wort (*Blackstonia perfoliata*), felwort (*Gentiana amarella*), centaury (*Centaurium minus*) and Autumn ladies tresses (*Spiranthes spiralis*), and perhaps most exciting of all the wild gladiolus (*Gladiolus illyricus*) which has several well established stations in the Forest. In a few places wild garlic or ramsons (*Allium ursinum*) grows thickly.

STREAMS AND BOGS

On the west side of the Forest where the highlands fall quickly to the Avon Valley, the streams are fast running and so have not such an interesting and varied flora as the streams on the east and south. There the streams and rivers flow through fairly flat land and their slow rate of flow enables a good deal of vegetation to grow in them—some of them getting quite choked up in the Summer. The result is that after heavy and continuous rain these streams overflow and form large areas of bog which are full of interest to the botanist. There are also quite a number of ponds of a small size—and a few large ones—which are very fertile, but which are apt to dry out wholly or partially in a hot summer when you can sometimes come across the curious sight of waterlilies flourishing in what looks like a grass field. The streams are gay in the Summer with masses of crowfoot (*Ranunculus aquatilis* and *R. hederaceus*), yellow waterlily (*Nupharlutea*), yellow flag (*Iris pseudacorus*), purple loosestrife (*Lythrum salicaria*) and the great water plantain (*Alisma plantago-aquatica*). In the spring there are drifts of blue of the water forget-me-not (*Myosotis palustris*). Some of the small, shallow streams are choked with the yellow bog St. John's wort (*Hypericum elodes*), and in the clearer pools can be found the three bladderworts (*Utricularia vulgaris*, which is rare, and *U. intermedia* and *U. minor*, which are more frequent): they are not easy to see as they are mostly submerged, but can be found when their slender yellow flowers come up a few inches out of the water. It is worthwhile to examine the whole plant, as the submerged stems are covered with little bladders: these bladders are traps that catch small water organisms which cannot escape again, and when they die they provide food material for the plant.

The three bur-reeds are found here, the branched (*Sparganium ramosum*) and the simple (*S. simplex*) being quite common and very conspicuous, standing up to two or three feet out of the water, while the small bur-reed (*S. minimum*) is less frequent and can easily be distinguished from the other two by its leaves which float on the surface of the water. There are innumerable small bogs all over the Forest but perhaps the largest and most interesting botanically are the areas of water-logged land which form Denny and Matley Bogs, those on each side of the railway line from Lyndhurst Road Station to Beaulieu Road Station on the east side of the Forest, Holmsley or Wilverley Bog below Holmsley Camp on the south west, and Hincheslea Bog on the south west of Brockenhurst. These bogs are deep and soft and great care should be taken when botanizing in them as they are rather dangerous for you can sink in quite a long way—when it is difficult to get yourself out again. However, a good deal of bog can be examined quite safely.

The bushes of bog myrtle or sweet gale (*Myrica gale*) are abundant and so is the cotton grass (*Eriophorum angustifolium*). The slender cotton grass (*E. gracile*) is also present but very rare. The bog asphodel (*Narthecium ossifragum*) makes a great show both in summer, when its golden flowers light up large areas of bog, and also in the autumn when the orange seed pods are caught in the sunlight. In quite a number of the drier bogs the beautiful marsh gentian (*Gentiana pneumonanthe*) is plentiful in late summer—sometimes so plentiful that the whole area looks quite blue. It does, however, have good and bad years and it is sometimes quite hard to find. Another of the Gentian family found in damp parts is the tiny *Cicendia filiformis* with bright yellow flowers which are seldom as much as a quarter of an inch across and are almost impossible to find unless it is a sunny day when the petals do open wide. Another very small flower of interest found on damp sandy parts is the *Illecebrum verticillatum* which trails along the ground and has rings of tiny white flowers all along the stem: it used to be very rare but for some years past it has been steadily on the increase. It is found mostly on damp sandy tracks, or bare patches, by ponds, as it seems unable to compete with other vegetation. Where lumps of sphagnum moss appear it is always worth looking at them closely as the pale yellow-green bog orchid (*Hammarbya paludosa*) may be growing there. This small orchid grows in many parts of the Forest, always on sphagnum, and always hard to see as it is small, only two or three inches high and very much the same colour as the surrounding vegetation.

A few of the ponds hold stands of the handsome great spearwort (*Ranunculus lingua*) which is the largest of our ranunculus, growing to at least four feet high, sometimes on its own and sometimes amongst reeds: the bright yellow flowers can be two inches across. Many of these ponds are full of white waterlily (*Nymphaea alba*), and buckbean (*Menyanthes trifoliata*) whose spikes of fringed, white flowers with bright pink buds stand up above the dark green leaves. Another Forest speciality is to be found in a few ponds—the rare *Ludwigia palustris* which has its only English station in the New Forest: it used to be found in Sussex too, but seems to have died out there: its small rather transparent-looking greenish flowers are not very easy to see and so do not make the rambler want to pick it.

Two of the sundews are plentiful in all bogs and damp places—the round-leaved (*Drosera rotundifolia*) and the oblong (*D. intermedia*) are usually found growing together and look very attractive when the sticky fluid on the red hairs round their leaves sparkles in the sun. These hairs close over insects which land on the leaves and inject fluid into them which kills them and makes them readily digestible by the plant. The third sundew (*D. anglica*) is rare in the Forest being found in only a few bogs: it is, of course, much more frequent further north. To see these sundew flowers really out it is probably best to look for them on a sunny morning when one small white flower on the flower spike will open for a few hours—a fresh one opening most days.

One of the butterworts (*Pinguicula lusitanica*)—another insectivorous plant—occurs mostly on shingly borders of ponds, as does also the marsh clubmoss (*Lycopodium inundatum*) and more commonly the bright pink flowers on the trailing stems of the bog pimpernel (*Anagallis tenella*) can be found. One other bog plant which used to be well established in a few places is the summer ladies tresses

(*Spiranthes aestivalis*): it is now very rare and seems to have practically vanished from its old haunts, but may turn up again there or in other bogs, as orchids are apt to do.

SEA SHORE

In times gone by the Forest came down to the sea shore for many miles, but now it only includes one stretch of about six miles on the Solent from the west side of Beaulieu river to Tanners Lake, just short of the Lymington river. We can also include both banks of the Beaulieu River from the mouth to the village of Beaulieu, which is tidal, and has a martime vegetation. Along this foreshore is to be found quite a varied flora. The most obvious plant is the cord grass (*Spartina townsendii*) which covers acres of the mud marsh land. This grass is a hybrid of *S. stricta* and *S. alterniflora* and since it was first noticed in Southampton Water about 1878 it has spread rapidly, not only locally, but also round the coast of England wherever suitable mud flats occur. Along the edge of the woods that come down to the sea shore can be found the stinking iris (*Iris foetidissima*), with its rather inconspicuous, mauvish flower and its brilliant orange-coloured seeds which show up when the ripe pods split. It is sometimes known as the roast beef plant as the stalks when broken smell strongly of roast beef. Another plant which spreads to the sandy shore is the burnet rose (*Rosa spinosissima*); it is covered with very sharp prickles and the cream coloured flowers have a lovely scent. Clumps of sea bladder campion (*Silene maritima*), sea beet (*Beta maritima*) and sea purslane (*Halimione portulacoides*) are to be found everywhere. The sea beet is still picked when young and eaten as spinach. A few plants of the charming, though prickly, grey-blue sea holly (*Eryngium maritimum*) are to be seen on the sandy shore above high water mark. Sea lavender (*Limonium vulgare*) and sea aster (*Aster tripolium*) both have good colonies here, while the thrift (*Armeria maritima*) grows amongst the short turf near the shore. Scurvy grass (*Cochlearia*), in several forms, abounds. An introduced shrub which has quite naturalized itself along this shore is the Duke of Argyll's tea tree (*Lycium halimifolium*): it grows abundantly and forms thick clumps. Other plants of interest along the shore are the sea milkwort (*Glaux maritima*) which is quite abundant, and the much less frequent spring vetch (*Vicia lathyroides*), subterranean clover (*Trifolium subterraneum*), hare's foot clover (*T. arvense*), English stone crop (*Sedum anglicum*), sheep's bit (*Jasione montana*) and the horned poppy (*Glaucium flavum*).

GRASSES AND SEDGES

For those botanists interested in grasses and sedges there are a fair number to be found. Townsend's *Flora of Hampshire* lists between thirty and forty. This Flora, which is old—the last edition is 1904—is still of great help to anyone exploring the Forest; even though some of the information may be out of date, it still gives a very good picture of what may be found.

FERNS

The ferns are plentiful and varied, growing by the streams, on banks and even on trees. At one time the Royal fern (*Osmunda regalis*) was to be found in quantities, but it has almost been lost to the Forest through people digging it up and planting it in their own gardens. There are, of course, local byelaws protecting the plants but unfortunately the area is so large that unscrupulous people still selfishly remove any plant that takes their fancy, never thinking that others might like to see, and enjoy, them in their natural surroundings.

There are many more wild flowers to be found in the Forest than are listed here, but perhaps this description of some of the flora will give you an idea of how rich an area it is from the botanical point of view, and how well worthwhile it is to explore at all times of the year.

Nightingale

The Lymington River, near Bolderford Bridge, Brockenhurst

The Fire Look-out Tower on Lyndhurst Hill, near Emery Down; seventy-five feet high

Commoners' pigs rooting for acorns

Forest Ponies and Cattle Grazing beside Bolton's Bench, Lyndhurst

Scots Pines in Highland Water Inclosure

Pollard Beeches at Soarley

There is a pleasure in the pathless woods,
There is a rapture on the lonely shore,
There is society, where none intrudes,
By the deep sea, and music in its roar;
I love not man the less, but Nature more,
From these our interviews . . .

BYRON

THE HISTORY OF THE FOREST WOODLANDS

BY D. W. YOUNG

THE latest survey by the Forestry Commission shows that the total area of woodland belonging to the Crown in the Forest is 31,432 acres. In this chapter we want to talk about these woods. They surely, more than any other part of it, give the Forest its unique character. Open heaths it is true have a beauty of their own, particularly in the late summer when heather is in bloom. They, however, form part of a much larger area which stretches in an ever narrowing tongue through the partially built up area north of Bournemouth and Poole to Wareham and ten to fifteen miles beyond, including the "Egdon Heath" country, which Hardy made famous. On those bright limpid days which come to us in spring, or in the late summer when the heaths and heather are in bloom, you can tramp across them with an amazing sense of joy and freedom, but in those almost more frequent days when the sun never pierces the clouds, there is nothing in the vegetation to relieve the drabness of the scenery. Even the distant views are lost in mist or haze and there creeps over you a depression, that sense of pessimism which places the beauty of nearly all Hardy's books in the minor key.

How different is the New Forest. It may be raining hard on a day in early November. The Forest heaths share all the drabness of those in Dorset. The ponies and cattle stand in misery with their backs to the wind. A steamy mist cuts off the distant view. Suddenly you come to a place where the woods reach down to the road, and straight ahead there is a path or rather a tunnel of gold for you; a fairyland of browns and yellows. Or it may be winter when the leaves have fallen from the trees and gather in hollows in the ground below, making a patchwork of browns, greys and greens, while overhead the branches of the trees interweave in a delicate tracery against the sky, picked out by the greys, greens and yellows of the lichens. Or again, it may be early spring when the bursting birch and larch buds blot out some of that tracery in a gentle haze of yellow and emerald green.

In high summer, when the trees are in full leaf of a darker hue, the woods taken on a more sombre aspect, but where, as often happens, there is a break in the canopy and a shaft of sunlight streams through on to a lichen-stained stem of an old gnarled beech, you are confronted with a beauty of more dramatic character which takes your breath away. It is just that kaleidoscopic changeableness of the woods—the fact that they are never quite the same for two days or even two hours together—which makes them the joy that they are. Quite apart from their own intrinsic beauty the woods have another interest in that they are the home of the deer, the badgers and squirrels, and many of the birds, reptiles and insects. You will not see much of them if you visit the woods in large chattering parties. Walking by yourself or with a friend who does not need to chatter, you will realise that the woods are not so devoid of animal life as you thought; the sight of a small herd of deer or a fine buck at the end of a ride is sufficient to make the whole day's excursion memorable.

We are so used to looking on our forests as a source of timber that we find it hard to realize that in William the Conqueror's day that was quite a secondary consideration, if considered at all. The paramount care of those who looked after the Forest was the protection of the deer and everything that the deer needed. This last included vert great and small, or in other words, timber and underwood.

These were not protected for their own sake but as shelter for the deer. So long as that shelter was not seriously interfered with, it is not supposed that the powers-that-be worried very much. It is quite certain that as the centuries passed and the population grew, the demand for material for houses grew apace. First for simple hovels of wattle and daub for which underwood was required, and later for more elaborate structures in which timber was used to a very considerable extent.

Whether legal or not, this led to cutting in the Royal Forests on a considerable scale; the discovery that once trees were cut the deer and the Commoners' animals never allowed the underwood to shoot again or the seedling beech and oak to grow, led to the first tree-growing enactment in the country being passed in 1483. It was not a very recondite measure. In a Royal Forest, enclosure of any kind was illegal—it interfered with the deer. The Act of 1483 made it legal, where the coppice had been cut on an area, for a ditch to be dug and a bank thrown up around that area and planted with thorns. In other words to enclose it with a quick hedge and leave it so enclosed for seven years or until such time that the coppice and seedlings were safe from grazing animals.

Considerable advantage was taken of that Act, and in the days of Queen Elizabeth I, when a census was taken of these encoppicements as they were called, a total of 5,800 acres was found, and there is evidence that this did not take into account a large number which had been thrown open and lost sight of.

This census is important because when the Act of 1698 in the reign of William III was passed, with a view to making good some of the depredations which had been allowed to happen to the Forest in the reigns of Charles I and II, the figure of 6,000 acres was borne in mind. The Act provided for the immediate planting of 2,000 acres and of a further 200 acres per annum for twenty years, making 6,000 acres in all. It also, for the first time, gave statutory recognition of Common Rights in the Forest. It provided a golden opportunity of putting the Forest in order, but it met with violent opposition. Only 1,022 acres were planted in the first fifteen years, a further 230 acres in 1750, and 2,044 acres in 1776. This last year was one of feverish activity in the Forest; this is interesting because it was in July of that year that the American colonies declared their independence. Britain was building up her Indian Empire too. Perhaps, with the need for an ever-growing navy, people saw the red light of decreasing growing stocks of oaks in the country's woodlands.

One development of this year was of particular interest. Scots pine was introduced into the Forest in 1776. The planting was confined to two small plots, one in Ocknell and the other in Bolderwood, but it was destined to bring a great change to the Forest and the surrounding country. Before that date no conifers had been introduced into the Forest or its environs. Within less than seventy years the pine was to show itself the species most at home in the Forest, regenerating itself naturally everywhere. Since then a number of other species of conifers have been introduced, at first merely as specimen trees, but later on a bigger scale, and some at least promise to be equally at home as the pine.

There was one other important feature about this statute of 1698 which has an important bearing on the subsequent development of the Forest. This was that it provided the Crown with what later came to be known as the "rolling power" of afforestation. It provided that when the Crown had planted the 6,000 acres, and the plants thereon had grown to a size at which they would be safe from grazing animals, these areas could be thrown open and a further like area enclosed and planted.

Britain's world-wide commitments were then steadily expanding, and with them the need for an ever larger and stronger navy. This need drew attention to the devastated condition of most of the English woods, the source of oak from which our warships were built at that time. Not unnaturally this was a matter of great concern. One wise and important step taken by the Government was the appointment of a Royal Commission:

> "to enquire into the state and condition of the woods, forests and land revenues of the Crown."

This Commission issued its first report in 1787, and its fifth, which dealt with the New Forest, in 1789. This report contained certain valuable recommendations, but the Government apparently postponed action upon them until the Commission's investigations were complete, and that was not until they had issued their last and seventeenth report in 1793. Recommendations included the reorganization of the government of the Forest and a continuation of the work under the rolling powers provided for in the Act of 1698.

There was some doubt about the legal position then, and a Bill extending the Crown's powers of enclosure was passed by the House of Commons, but thrown out by the Lords. Finally the provisions of the Act of 1698 were re-enacted in 1808. The planting programme was vigorously carried out and by 1848 some 7,000 acres had been planted and were reported mainly in very good condition. The object, of course, was oak for the Navy; some of the early plantings were of pure oak but, later on, considerable areas were planted with Scots pine nurses. The oaks and pines were set four feet apart in alternate rows the same distance apart. Most of the pines in these early plantations were removed quite young and sold for the most part as pit props. Very few were allowed to grow to maturity and most that were so allowed were left as belts around the outside of the plantations. Godshill, which was planted in 1810, is an example; and the old pines standing along the edge of that Inclosure are over 150 years old now. As will be seen, this practice was not so rigorously followed in later plantations, but before we deal with the very extensive plantations made between 1850 and 1865 we must consider another matter.

As has already been made clear, the whole object of a Royal Forest was to provide sport for the king in the hunting of deer. All sovereigns up to James II appear to have taken advantage of these facilities. Later sovereigns appear in the main to have left the Officers of the Crown to do the hunting, and in the end to look merely on the forests as a source of venison. It is not surprising in these circumstances that the head of deer in the Forest became very large, and complaints by the Commoners became increasingly vocal during the first half of the nineteenth century.

The matter came to a head in the Report of the Select Committee of 1848. Negotiations were entered into with a group of Commoners who were believed to represent the whole of them. As a result of these negotiations an Act, known as the Deer Removal Act, was passed in 1851 under which the deer were ordered to be destroyed, and in compensation the Crown was authorized to enclose 10,000 acres more for timber production. This increased the area which the Crown could keep enclosed at any one time to 16,000 acres. But the Crown still claimed the right to the "rolling powers" which have already been referred to, and that sowed seeds for trouble in the future. Mr. Cumberbatch, the Deputy Surveyor of that day, then a young man of twenty-five or twenty-six years, tackled the task with vigour, and he had 4,000 acres cleared, fenced, and planted within the first year or so. Protests, however, grew in frequency and volume as the work proceeded. These protests came from two classes of people, who, when they got together, made a fairly formidable front. On the one hand there were the Commoners who foresaw that if the "rolling powers" were carried to an extreme their rights would become valueless; there was some justification for this fear, as a letter from Mr. Cumberbatch, the Deputy Surveyor of 1853, had been published with a Report made by a Select Committee of 1868, in which he recommended that the "rolling powers" should be exercised to the full.

The other class of protesters were the people who had come to live in the Forest because of its beauty. They hated to see large areas being cleared of the old pollard oaks and beeches. Pollards, it must be understood, are trees which have had their tops cut off at some time, six feet to ten feet from the ground, and allowed to shoot again. Beech and oak in the Forest were pollarded to provide food for the deer in the winter. The branches cut were left lying on the ground and the deer nibbled off the bark. In the old days one of the perquisites of the keepers was to have the branchwood after the deer had had the bark. Here was a clear temptation to pollard more trees than were necessary for the deer, and thus prevent many oaks from growing to Navy timber size. Further pollarding was made illegal in the Act of 1698, so the pollards we see today must be of considerable age—270 years at least. At this age, they are not so easily recognised as pollards. Five, six or even more branches spring out from where the top was cut off and have generally grown to the size of trees themselves. Examples may be seen in nearly all the woods of the open Forest; Mark Ash, Ridley and Denny Wood are notable examples. These old pollards are lovely old things, just the type that Rackham used to love to paint and draw in his fairy books. They are however of little value as timber, and trees which have not been pollarded but allowed to grow to their full stature have an awesome beauty of their own. Small patches of these may be seen in the old woods. Younger examples are growing up in some of the Inclosures—for instance in the eastern end of Shave Green.

At the time when the Deer Removal Act was passed, ironclads were rapidly replacing the old wooden ships and the need for Navy timber was not so urgent. Apart from that, it was realised that these much larger areas would take some of the woodlands on to inferior soil unfit for hardwoods. It was therefore expressly provided in the Act that species other than oak could be planted. As a result not only was oak planted with Scots pine nurses, but some Inclosures were planted with pure pine. This was the time of the biggest incursion of conifers in the Forest. It is not very clear whether with intention or from neglect—probably the latter—a different method of treatment was given the areas of oak with pine nurses to that given earlier in the nineteenth century. Then the pine nurses were cut out at a very early age, but in these later plantations they were allowed to stand much longer. Indeed in some cases they were not cut out at all. As a result, particularly on those sites where the soil was less suited to the oak, the nurses overlaid the baby. Many of the pure stands of pine today owe their origin to this fact. The old pine stands in Busketts Inclosure are a case in point. On the other hand, at the eastern end of Shave Green already referred to there is an example of a case where the soil was good and the oak able to keep pace with the pine. Many of the pines were left as late as 1932. Indeed in Shave Green you will find examples of both. As you walk westwards along the Douglas fir avenue the quality of the soil falls off, and about the middle of the Inclosure you come upon pure stands of pine where the pines have suppressed the oak.

The controversy over the plantings under the Deer Removal Act grew in intensity as the years went by. These early plantings could not have been very pretty for the trees had to be planted in straight rows to facilitate weeding. There was, at the time, growing apprehension about the beauty of the Forest, and feeling on this matter intensified the opposition to the work.

In 1868 a Select Committee was appointed to go into the matter. They heard many witnesses and reported that never could there be peace between Crown and Commoners under the existing arrangements, and recommended that like so many other commons and forests the New Forest should be enclosed. This arrangement, though it would have destroyed the Forest as we know it, would have secured a much larger area for afforestation. A Bill carrying out the Committee's recommendations was submitted to Parliament, but met with so much opposition that it was dropped before the second reading. The Commoners also drafted a Bill on much the same lines but that was never introduced to Parliament. In 1871 a resolution was passed by the House of Commons that there should be no more cutting of old trees or making new enclosures in the New Forest pending a settlement of the whole question, and in 1875 another Select Committee was appointed. This Committee suggested an entirely different solution, and the New Forest Act of 1877 gave effect to its recommendations. Under this Act the Crown gave up its rolling powers and no more land could be enclosed beyond what had been enclosed in the reign of William III and subsequently up to the passing of this Act.

The legal position of the woods as determined by the Acts of 1877, 1949 and 1964 is set out under "Land Areas" on page 95.

The New Forest Act, 1949, brought about some very important changes. The most important of these have to do with the Verderers, with whom we are more particularly concerned in a later chapter, but for the sake of completeness it will be perhaps as well to mention them briefly here.

Under the 1949 Act there are now ten Verderers, five being appointed and five elected. The Official Verderer is appointed by the Queen and one Verderer each is appointed by the Forestry Commissioners, the Minister of Agriculture, the local planning authority, and the Council for the Preservation of Rural England. The remaining five Verderers are elected by the Commoners. For this purpose a Commoner is defined as an occupier (not necessarily the owner) of not less than one acre of land to which common rights are attached. Of the total number of ten Verderers, only the Official

Verderer, and four others nominated by the Lord Chancellor can sit and adjudicate in the Court of Swainmote. All other matters are considered and decided upon by all the Verderers, except that in any division upon the question of allowing the Forestry Commissioners or the Minister of Agriculture to enclose lands in the Open Forest for purposes defined by the Act, the appointee of the authority concerned is not allowed to vote.

The only effective source of revenue which the Verderers had under the 1877 Act was what are called marking fees, i.e. the charge made when an animal is turned out in the Forest. This was fixed by the Act at a maximum of 2*s*. 6*d*. per head per annum and provided funds quite inadequate for the Verderers' needs. Under the 1949 Act no maximum is fixed, and, subject to the approval of the Minister of Agriculture, the Verderers can fix the marking fees to meet their needs. In addition, they are authorised to permit the Forestry Commissioners to enclose and afforest areas not exceeding a total of 5,000 acres. For this they charge by way of compensation a yearly rent of 4*s*. per acre. It is hoped by this means to keep the marking fees at as low a level as possible.

There is one other provision which ought to be mentioned because it has a direct bearing on the woodlands of the Forest. The area of what has been described as "Ancient and Ornamental woods" was assessed in 1963 at 7,487 acres. Under the 1877 Act the Forestry Commissioners had no power to do anything in these woods. This was rather tragic because nearly every winter a heavy snowstorm or gale brings a number of the ancient monarchs crashing to the ground. Cattle and ponies, on the other hand, keep any natural regeneration closely grazed back. This means that the area of completely stocked woods has dwindled year by year. To allow these woods to disappear would constitute an irreparable loss. Under the 1949 Act, subject to the approval of the Verderers, the Forestry Commissioners may enclose an area not exceeding twenty acres in any one place and reafforest it. Special care for amenities is taken in this work and plantations are kept enclosed until the risk of damage by animals has ceased.

THE NEW FOREST ACT, 1964

The new organisation under the 1949 Act, described by Mr. D. W. Young above, made possible many improvements in the control of the Forest's woodlands and grazing livestock. But it was found in practice that further powers were needed. Changes were desirable, too, in the boundaries of the Forest. These improvements were made possible by a further Act of Parliament in 1964.

The main provisions of this Act are as follows:

(1) The "perambulation" or legal boundary of the Forest was altered so as to exclude certain lands, mainly on the south and east, and to include others, chiefly in the north and west. A main object of these changes was to allow better control of wandering livestock, by better barriers. The new boundaries are shown in the map on the front endpaper of this Guide.

(2) Powers were granted for the fencing-in of the main road, A.35, from Southampton through Lyndhurst to Bournemouth, so as to reduce the risk of accidents due to wandering ponies.

(3) Powers were granted for the construction of cattle grids across public roads where they enter the Forest, so as to restrict the ponies from leaving their grazing grounds, whilst at the same time allowing free entrance for vehicles.

(4) Provision was made for the creation of permanent camping sites.

(5) The Forestry Commission was given further powers to replant and tend the "ornamental woods" which contribute so much to the Forest's landscape. A further 500 acres may, if necessary, be fenced in for purposes of regeneration.

Most of the changes foreshadowed by this Act have already been put into operation, with the requisite co-operation and approval of the Verderers.

Timber Hauling

Till from the breathing lawns a forest springs
Of youth, integrity and loveliness . . .

SHELLEY

THE FORESTER'S TASK

BY W. A. CADMAN

No forest in Britain has easier access for the general public than the New Forest. Many thousands of visitors come every year, some to picnic, some to walk, some to camp overnight. Few realize the amount of work which goes on all the year round in the forest: work which is needed to maintain the forest trees, the amenities, the grazing in the Open Forest and the conservation of wild life.

Very broadly, the New Forest can be divided into three categories of land use.

THE OPEN FOREST

There is the Open Forest where the Commoners' animals and the public have the right to roam at large. If this area was left entirely alone the greater part of it would become grown over and useless for grazing. Every year selected areas of coarse vegetation have to be cut or burnt to prevent this from happening. Some 1,000 acres are so treated annually, the work being carried out by the forest keepers, after prior consultation with the Verderers of the New Forest and the Nature Conservancy. On the Open Forest, bridges and animal crossing places have to be maintained and water courses kept free from blockages. The removal of ragwort is quite a large and costly annual job. Some areas are cut by machine.

The clearance of litter bins is another task which requires careful organisation. The litter team, using vehicles specially equipped for refuse collection, travels 100 miles a day and during holiday periods a 12-hour day is worked. Apart from the old cars which are dumped in the forest, 800 tons of litter are collected annually.

ANCIENT AND ORNAMENTAL WOODS

On the Open Forest there are certain woodlands which are unenclosed, known as the Ancient and Ornamental Woods. This, then, is the second category. Here grow great beech trees and gnarled old oaks, many of which were pollarded more than 270 years ago. For this practice of cutting off the branches in winter in order to provide fodder for the deer, and fuel for the local populace, was stopped by law 270 years ago, when it was realized that it was most harmful to the quality of the timber. However, as described in the previous chapter, the forester was not allowed to fell timber in these areas, unless it was windblown or decayed. Moreover, as animals are free to graze under these ancient trees, many of the natural seedlings which germinate are eaten. The result is that many of the older beechwoods are fast becoming derelict.

However, there is a continuous but slow change. In many areas scrub and holly develop, and these protect young seedlings of the major species which grow up through the scrub.

The 1949 and 1964 Acts allow the felling and regeneration of areas up to twenty acres within the general area of the Ancient and Ornamental woodlands, subject to the Verderers' approval.

Where possible the forester encourages natural regeneration from the original crop. But where this is impossible, because the mother trees do not bear seed, or because the seedlings are killed by mice, squirrels or deer, or by competition with dense vegetation, then the forester has to plant other trees, using mainly broadleaved species.

In practice, the twenty-acre fellings that are permissible have proved too large for the best results. Heavy opening of the canopy causes too drastic a wind effect on those trees that remain. In future, blocks averaging 350 acres in size will be thinned out carefully, each being treated every twenty years to encourage natural re-growth of young trees.

When these new plantings within the Ancient and Ornamental blocks have grown sufficiently to be safe from grazing animals, then all fences will be taken down again.

INCLOSURES

In contrast to the Open Forest and to the Ancient and Ornamental woodland areas there is the third category, consisting of the various Inclosures. Here the forester's main object is to practise good forestry and to grow commercially valuable timber, whilst still paying keen attention to the amenities of the forest.

Let us take a look at the work which the forester has to carry out in the Inclosures. Up to 1959 there had been no new enclosure of Open Forest for over one hundred years. However, under the 1949 Act, powers were granted for 5,000 acres of Open Forest to be enclosed, subject to agreement by the Verderers. The first of these agreed enclosures—known as the Verderers' Inclosures—are sited at Dunces Arch, Markway, Fletchers Thorns, Dibden, Marchwood, Fawley, Longdown, Dur Hill, Turf Hill and Holbury. A main reason for choosing these sites was to prevent grazing animals from straying on to the most dangerous roads, or outside the perambulation of the forest. In making these new Inclosures the first necessity was a stockproof fence, and as it was agreed to provide re-seeded areas around the new Inclosures, to compensate the Commoners for the loss of the larger areas of rough grazing within the Inclosures, a second fence has been necessary to protect the re-seeded strips.

Before planting, main watercourses had to be drained with a mechanical excavator and then the whole area ploughed at 5½ ft. spacing with crawler tractors and special ploughs. Ploughing was necessary for three reasons: to improve drainage, to aerate the soil and to eliminate vegetation. On the worst soils, that is the compact gravels which often have an underlying iron pan, a subsoiler was used behind the plough in order to break the pan. During the winter months, planting took place with young trees which had been specially grown in forest nurseries. It was necessary to plant the correct species on the different types of soil, bearing in mind that, to grow well, hardwoods require the best soil conditions, just as wheat can only be grown on the best farm land, although conifers will grow on soil unsuitable even for oats. However, in the New Forest hardwoods are given a wider range than normal, because of the high regard paid to amenity. Fashions change. Nowadays it is the custom to plant a wide, irregular belt of hardwoods on the outside edge in order to screen the conifers. A hundred years ago a belt of conifers was often planted on the outside of the hardwoods, in order to protect them!

Like most of the poor acid soils in Britain, the New Forest soil is very deficient in phosphate, therefore a small application of this mineral was given to each tree at the time of planting.

During the following summer, weed growth (bracken, coarse grass, etc.) had to be watched and when necessary cut back.

Thus is a forest Inclosure made.

A forester's task is to plant, tend and care for the young trees, in due course favouring the best stems by removing the worst—those which are badly shaped or which have grown coarsely.

This process is called thinning, and starts somewhere between the fifteenth and twentieth years. Thus some 1,750 young trees per acre are planted, but only 80 to 100 per acre reach maturity: these are the best stems, straight, clean and free from dead knots. The rest are removed during the periodic thinnings providing poles, which are saleable and yield a financial return. Conifers are ready for the final felling at from 60 to 80 years, but hardwoods require 120 years.

NATURAL REGENERATION

The warm summers and light soils of the New Forest are particularly favourable for the natural regeneration of almost every tree species which will grow in this part of the world. In the past this method of renewing tree crops was often applied to good effect. Sufficient mother trees were left standing to seed up the soil laid bare by felling the rest of the crop, the mother trees being removed at a later stage when the new crop was firmly established. Such natural regeneration of oak may be seen at Salisbury Trench, sycamore at Denny Inclosure, beech almost everywhere, where there are mother trees, which will seed on to ground enclosed against animals. Douglas fir regeneration is widespread, but is seen at its best at Bolderwood. Norway spruce is present at Puck Pits and silver fir at New Park. Sitka spruce is regenerating freely in Knightwood, and Corsican pine under the magnificent belt along the Knightwood-Burley road. The best examples of Scots pine regeneration followed the war-time fellings of 1939/45 in Busketts and Parkhill Inclosures and in many places elsewhere. Often a mixture of different species comes up together, and may be retained as such or reduced to one kind.

Today, however, the forester has available improved strains of timber trees that promise higher yields than the unselected specimens that made up the previous crop. Or he may wish to change the kind of tree to a more profitable one. Replanting has, therefore, become the usual means of replacing felled crops.

HARVESTING

The ultimate aim of planting trees commercially is to harvest and market the various products with the maximum profit.

The first produce comes from thinnings—the removal of inferior stems in order to give space to the better ones remaining, which here in the New Forest is done somewhere between the fifteenth and twentieth years with fast-growing conifers. Hardwoods cannot be thinned until they are much older, and hardwood thinnings rarely have a profitable sale value.

Different timber crops reach the age for best financial return at differing ages. Two, sometimes three, crops of the more profitable conifers may be grown in the same period that it takes to grow one hardwood crop. Moreover, hardwoods need the best soils to produce good quality timber and only good quality hardwood timber is readily saleable. These factors explain the preference of foresters for the conifers on the, generally poor, New Forest soils.

For various reasons a high proportion of the timber in the New Forest has been kept standing well beyond the period for the highest financial returns. Therefore felling the oldest crops is necessary as part of the process of harvesting: and usually replacement must be by the most valuable species, except where amenity considerations have precedence. Harvesting in the New Forest is designed to give a high production of pulpwood, that is small logs suitable for making into paper or into packages, such as food cartons for sales in shops, cigarette packets, and so forth. Telegraph poles and round logs for the sawmills, both conifer and hardwood, are the other principal items of production, while fencing materials are supplied to local farmers.

Felling is nowadays done with power saws, and the hauling out ofall this timber is largely mechanised. An efficient or ganisation of all transport has been developed to keep the huge loads of pulpwood flowing to the carton board mills in accordance with the annual contract.

FOREST KEEPERS' DUTIES

The Forest Keepers' duties are roughly divided between the enforcement of the Forestry Commission Byelaws—(and civil offences, since the keepers are also special constables)—and the humane but necessary control of deer and other animals which cause damage.

Deer have to be controlled because of the damage they can do to forest, farms, and even gardens. Further, if they were allowed to increase without any restriction, their food supply would not hold out during the lean months of the year and deaths through starvation would ensue. Control is done by rifle, selectively and humanely, in accordance with a detailed plan.

New Forest keepers are on duty all the time. Often they are out until long after dark on night patrols for poachers. Checking camping permits is a huge task, and many an inexperienced camper has benefited from the kindly advice of a keeper.

FIRE RISK

Of all the many tasks of the forester there is one only which is thoroughly unenviable—that of fire-fighting. During Bank Holidays and fine week-ends, when a warm wind blows and all the world likes to get out and about in the spring sunshine, the forester is a very worried man. There is no holiday for him—unless it rains! He is on call, day and night, wondering all the time just where some careless person will drop a cigarette, or lighted match. A such times the Fire Towers at Emery Down, Picket Post, Fritham and Dibden are fully manned. Teams of fire-fighters, equipped with wireless and water, stand by throughout the holiday. When the Fire Duty Officer can say "Stand down", without having had a fire incident, it has been a very good holiday.

Collared Dove, a newcomer to the Forest

It is often said that a forester never sees the result of his work. But when the sad day comes for him to retire, he can point with pride to many acres of tall trees, planted by himself as a young man, now growing where maybe there used to be none, and he will be well satisfied. For he knows that the forest will still be there long after his children's children are old men.

As he lights his pipe in the evening of his life, carefully snuffing the match by life-long habit, he may muse on the fact that the oak tree planted by himself on the roadside, may well have 15 million people, 15,000 deer, 150 Verderers, 50 Foresters and 15 Deputy Surveyors pass beneath its branches before its day is done!

An Aerial View of Lyndhurst, with the Queen's House seen to the left of the Church, and Northerwood House in the top right-hand corner

Beaulieu seen from the air, looking across the Beaulieu River to the Palace House and the Abbey ruins

A Forester goes on his rounds below the tall Corsican Pines of Knightwood

Brockenhurst Church

The Verderers' Hall, Lyndhurst

Roebuck

Shy as the squirrel and wayward as the swallow
Swift as the swallow along the river's light

MEREDITH

WILD ANIMALS AND BIRDS

BY OLIVER HOOK

A present-day description of the fauna of the New Forest would be incomplete without a brief reference to the past, as an indication of the marked changes that have taken place in this unique area during the last 900 years, and the part that man has played in bringing this about.

When William the Conqueror ordained that this relatively unproductive area should become one of the Royal Forests, to be preserved strictly for hunting by the King and his friends, the quarry according to that ancient document "Antiquas Britanniae", written before the Conquest, were the Beasts of the Forest, consisting of the Hart, the Hind, the Hare, the Boar and the Wolf. In addition there were the Beasts of the Chase, consisting of the Buck, the Doe, the Fox, the Marten and the Roe, and also the Beasts and Fowls of the Warren which were the Hare, the Coney, the Pheasant and the Partridge.

Manwood, in his Forest Laws, 1598, states "the beasts of the forest do make their abode, all the day time, in the great coverts and secret places in the woods: and in the night season they do repair into the lawnes, meadows, pastures and pleasant feedings, for their food and relief. And therefore they are called Silvesters, that is to say beasts of the wood. And the beasts of the Chase, they do make their abode all the day time in the fields and upon the hills where they may see round about them afar off, who doth stir or come near them: and in the night season when everybody is at rest and all is quiet then they do repair unto the corn-fields and valleys where the lawnes, meadows and pleasant feedings are for their food and relief, and therefore they are called Campestres". No doubt these animals were in far greater numbers 1,000 years ago than is the case today, but with the exception of the Wolf (extinct about A.D. 1500), the Boar (extinct about A.D. 1600), and the Marten (extinct during the nineteenth century), all are present in the New Forest today.

Under the harsh Forest Laws the inhabitants of the New Forest district, from the tenth century onwards, were forbidden to hunt any game within its perambulation, and the penalties for disobeying the provisions of this harsh Act might be blinding, or in extreme cases death.

Probably the best definition of a Royal Forest is given by Manwood in the XVI century, as follows: "A forest is a certain territory of woody grounds and fruitful pastures, privileged for wild beasts and fowls of forest, chase and warren to rest and abide in, in the safe protection of the king, for his princely delight and pleasure".

During successive reigns the Sovereigns continued to hunt in the New Forest, or to allow their friends to do so, according to individual preferences, and the administration continued to give first importance to the maintenance of an adequate head of beasts of the Forest and of the Chase, far on into the XV and XVI centuries. We know that in the year 1670 a census of deer within the perambulation disclosed a total of "7,593 Fallow Deere and 357 Red Deere", making 7,950 deer in all, but we are not told how the census was conducted, and we are aware of the difficulty of assessing populations of deer in woodland areas.

From Canute's day, down the centuries until the time of Charles II, hunting by those in Court circles was fairly regularly undertaken, and the management of the New Forest was conducted by the Verderers, Regarders, Agisters, Foresters, Woodwards, Stewards and others, each having his special official duties in respect of vert (growing trees and underwood), and venison (the beasts of the Forest and of the Chase). The deer were virtually paramount, and because of this, and as it was illegal to enclose land in the Forest and exclude the deer, certain local residents acquired rights of common over Crown land, whereby their cattle, ponies, pigs and other commonable animals could be depastured on the open wastes of the New Forest. But no domestic animals were supposed to roam at large, and compete with the deer, during the period of the Winter Heyning (22 November to 4 May) and the Fence Month (20th June to 20th July) when the deer were dropping their calves and fawns. Thus there remained barely 5½ months in each year during which the domestic animals could be turned out.

Japanese Sika Deer

DEER

With the passing of the New Forest Act, 1851, commonly called the Deer Removal Act, the Crown relinquished the right to keep deer in the New Forest in exchange for permission to enclose a further 10,000 acres for the purpose of growing timber. In consequence a large number of deer were killed, but they were never exterminated as the Act laid down, for the reason that as they were killed fresh stock came in from adjoining woods.

The present status of wild deer in the New Forest is that there are four species, Fallow, Roe, Japanese Sika and Red Deer, and their numbers are controlled by the Forestry Commission so that they shall not be allowed to become a nuisance to forestry or to agriculture.

With the possible exception of the Red Deer, of which there are now very few, the New Forest provides very nearly ideal conditions for deer. Being primarily woodland animals, they can find adequate cover for their own protection, and for breeding, in the 25,000 acres of broadleaved and coniferous woods, where they can browse on tree foliage, grasses, mosses and other vegetation, often grazing after dark on the adjacent lawns and heaths, but returning to the woods for the daylight hours. Some damage is certainly done by the bucks and stags during the rutting season and also when the "velvet" covering of the new antlers is being shed, and in both cases small trees and saplings are "frayed" by the deer, often resulting in the removal of essential bark and the destruction of the tree.

Deer may sometimes be seen at night in the headlights of a car, as they cross the roads in wooded areas, but it needs a knowledge of their habits, and some experience of stalking, before one can be sure of approaching deer during the daytime. The New Forest race of Fallow are interesting in that they have, during the summer months, a coat of light chestnut colour, spotted white, but in the winter this coat is changed to one of unspotted dark dun, with white belly, and they present an altogether different appearance after each moult, although the white tail with black covering is a distinctive feature at all seasons. Similarly the summer coat of the Roe, which is a bright foxy red, is moulted in the autumn and the winter coat of buff grey is assumed, with pure white caudal patch around the rudimentary tail. In the Japanese Sika, the spots that are present in the summer coat are lost in the winter coat. Occasionally one of the few white Fallow may be seen.

SMALLER BEASTS

If more space has been devoted to deer than to some of the smaller mammals, it is because of the greater chance of seeing them, for they are the largest of our wild animals resident in the Forest. The population of the Fox and the Badger, our two largest Carnivores, is well established, and many of the woods contain earths and sets in which these two species breed each spring. The Fox is hunted by the New Forest Hounds, and it is probably the fact that from the hunting point of view there are too many foxes. The Crown Keepers, whose duties demand of them a good knowledge of natural history and woodcraft, know where these animals can be seen, but, as with the deer, great care is necessary in approaching them if a close view is to be obtained.

Badger

The Otter is present in several of the New Forest streams, but it is a most difficult animal to see, being like the Badger a beast of the night. In the autumn the Otter follows the seatrout up to the spawning grounds in the headwaters of certain streams and during the hard weather they will drop back downstream to the estuaries, and to the Solent shore, where their feeding grounds are less likely to become frozen and where marine foods will constitute their main diet. A pack of Otter Hounds visit the New Forest during the summer months.

Of the remaining flesh-eating mammals, the Stoat and Weasel are present in small numbers that fluctuate within limits with the populations of their prey, and at infrequent intervals the Common Seal has visited the Beaulieu River and Southampton Water.

Among the Rodents, the Grey Squirrel has, since its first appearance here in January, 1940, now acquired the status of a major pest, and it is present everywhere in large numbers. Before its advent, the Red Squirrel was common, although subject to periodical outbreaks of disease that affected its numbers, but with the coming of the Grey Squirrel the smaller and more attractive Red species has now quite disappeared, and it is necessary to visit the Isle of Wight to see it. Fortunately the Grey Squirrel has not been released there. Harmful to forestry and agriculture alike, and omnivorous in its diet, the Grey Squirrel is relentlessly destroyed by the Crown Keepers, and great numbers are shot and trapped each year; nevertheless the population of these pests tends rather to increase than to diminish.

Few places in the Forest where trees are growing are free from visits by these unwanted and very agile animals which, because of their arboreal habits, have virtually no enemies apart from man, although a few are caught by foxes at ground level.

There can be few places in Britain where the Brown Rat is absent, and certainly the species is present in our district and, if allowed, it would in a very short time become abundant and a nuisance. Fortunately, the Local Authorities have an excellent service of pest control, that is available to ratepayers. To a lesser extent the same can be said of the House Mouse, but as so many of these mice harbour in corn ricks, and as cereals are very little grown in our area, the House Mouse is not unduly numerous.

The Field Mice and Voles, however, find in our woodlands, pastures, hedgerows and heaths habitats to their liking, and in some years they are numerous and widespread. In years when the beech and oak shed an abundance of seed, these small mammals may achieve a remarkable up-surge in population, and it has been known in "vole years" for th eShort-tailed Vole and the Bank Vole to inflict considerable damage t o young plantations of several species of trees, gnawing the bark and often causing the trees to die. Although these attacks are infrequent, they are difficult to combat, but luckily the excessive numbers of voles decrease almost as suddenly as they build up, and predators, disease and food shortage, soon bring population density down to normal. These sudden increases seldom apply to the aquatic Water Vole, which occurs in small numbers along the banks of several Forest streams.

The handsome Yellow-necked Field Mouse (*Apodemus flavicollis*) is established in several small colonies in the woodland areas, and like its near relative the Long-tailed Field Mouse, is liable to increase in times of food abundance and cause trouble in the garden. Domestic cats are constant predators of the mice and voles, and they must catch large numbers of them, and also of the shrews, of which we have three species, the Common, the Pigmy and the Water Shrew. Whilst it is sometimes possible to watch field mice and voles during the daytime, as they forage for food, care being taken to make no sudden movement to alarm them, the same cannot be said of the shrews, whose shrill voice can often be heard in the rank vegetation. These little creatures are fairly abundant, and the Water Shrew is often to be found long distances from water. Few animals will eat shrews, but the Barn and Tawny Owls will, and traces of all three species, as well as of the mice and voles, can be found in their pellets.

Our other two insectivores, the Mole and the Hedgehog, are both to be found in the area, the former throwing up the familiar molehills in open fields, and often working in the woods, and the hedgehogs often meeting their death as a result of their habit of using the roadways at night time.

Two other small rodents have become scarce in recent years in Hampshire—the Dormouse, that prefers the oakwoods with hazel coppice, where it constructs is spherical nest of grass and honeysuckle bine some three feet from the ground, and as winter approaches retires into another nest at the root of a clump of hazel and hibernates until the spring. And the tiny and attractive Harvest Mouse that also builds a spherical nest of grass in the cornfields or tall vegetation, and usually spends the winter months in the corn ricks and is found at threshing time in the spring.

Of the rabbit, the spread of myxomatosis, from 1954 onwards, claimed the bulk of our native population, but individuals escaped the disease, and but for the control of the Crown Keepers of the Forestry Commission they would soon build up their numbers again. When the rabbit nearly disappeared, the foxes turned their attention to other foods and ate more mice and voles, and many more beetles, than before, as has been proved by analyses of stomach contents.

The hare is hunted by the New Forest Beagles; since the decline in numbers of rabbits the population of hares has increased, and what is more interesting, hares have spread to parts of the Forest that they had not been known to frequent in previous years. They are now fairly well distributed, and are to be met with on most of our heaths and in many of our woodland areas at suitable seasons.

There remain, to complete our list of the mammals of the New Forest, the Bats, and it is interesting to record that eleven of the twelve species on the British List have been recorded here, including the rare Bechstein's Bat and the scarce Barbastelle; Leisler's bat is absent. The commonest bats, however, are the large Noctule, with a wing-span of 14 inches, the much smaller Pipistrelle, the Long-eared, Natterer's and the Whiskered Bat.

BIRDS

It is generally accepted that birds are easier to observe and study than mammals, although the student of each would have his own special reasons for selecting one or the other in the first instance. More work is being done today on birds by scientists and amateurs than ever before, and recorded observations are being classified by county representatives of organizations devoted entirely to the study of birds.

In an area of 144 square miles, such as the New Forest, with its varied topographical features, its woods and heaths, streams and bogs, estuaries and coastline, one can expect to find a number of

Dartford Warbler

species of birds, each associated with its own particular type of habitat. Those of us who live in the New Forest, and those who pay occasional visits, will soon learn which species to expect in different types of country. We will know, for example, our resident species, and when to expect those migrants that arrive in spring to breed with us, and those that are passing northwards to breed in higher latitudes. The latter are seen again on their return migration southwards in the late summer and autumn. Again, many species, especially the Geese, Ducks and Scandinavian Thrushes come south to us as winter visitors, returning northwards to nest in the spring. It is important that these seasonal movements should be appreciated and understood, and that an observer should know approximately when a particular species of bird may be expected, and in what type of country it is likely to establish its breeding territory.

The birds that come most easily before our notice are those of the garden, and in this category the district cannot be said to be lacking in any of the commoner species—Blackbird, the two Thrushes, Chaffinch, Greenfinch, Sparrow, Starling, Spotted Flycatcher, Tits, Robin, Swallow, Martin, Swift, Pied Wagtail, Hedge-Sparrow—all are present and well distributed. But where hornbeam is growing one may expect occasionally to see the massive-billed Hawfinch, and on the bird-table the Nuthatch, and perhaps the now-more-frequent Magpie, or even the Great Spotted Woodpecker.

Widening the area to include hedgerow and field, the birds one may expect to see, or hear, besides the commoner species, are Skylark, Cuckoo, Long-tailed Tit, Turtle Dove, Sparrow Hawk, Blackcap, and several other Warblers. The Nightingale can be heard in some districts, but it is absent from the Ancient and Ornamental woods, and from pinewoods, though numerous along both banks of the Beaulieu River where its beautiful and remarkable song can be heard by day and by night. The Barn Owl occurs on

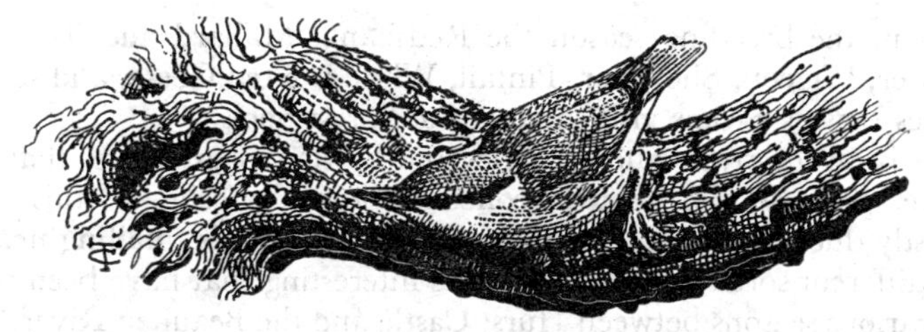

Nuthatch

some of the farmland, and near the coastal marshes, and that useful bird the Kestrel, and also the Little Owl, are by no means rare.

Visiting the deciduous woodlands we may expect to see Crow, Jay (much increased in numbers in recent years), Jackdaw, Tree Creeper, the various Leaf-Warblers, the three Woodpeckers, Tawny Owl, Woodcock and Buzzard. Ring Dove, Stock Dove, Collared Dove and the little migrant Turtle Dove are also well established as breeding species. In former years the Honey Buzzard bred in the more secluded woods; it may still visit us as a vagrant.

The species of birds to be found in the pure coniferous woods are few, and broadly are confined to the Long-eared Owl, Crossbill (which breeds locally), the tiny Goldcrest, Wood Pigeon, Crow and a few others. Conifers are necessary to our economy, as they provide the softwoods that Britain needs, and in times of national emergency must have at all costs. Moreover they are relatively fast-growing and give quicker returns of timber than do hardwoods. On some of the poorer soils conifers are the only trees than can be grown.

Proceeding to the open heaths, with or without gorse, we have in the Dartford Warbler—our only resident Warbler—a species that is susceptible to extreme cold, and in the winter of 1962/63 we lost nearly all of them in the hard weather, and this was also the case with the Stonechat, another bird of the heath, the Long-tailed Tit and some others. The Dartford Warbler population is now luckily building up again, but it is by no means abundant and will need careful protection. The Woodlark breeds here, but is very local and one always wishes that its melodious song could be more often heard. The Linnet, Tree and Meadow Pipits, Wheatear, Red-backed Shrike, Nightjar and, in the nesting season the Curlew, may all be found upon our heaths, as also may, if you are lucky enough to see it, the Montagu's Harrier and that beautiful little falcon the Hobby.

By pond and stream we have the Grey and the Yellow Wagtails, Sedge Warbler, Reed Bunting, Kingfisher (which in winter repairs to the saltings), Heron, Great Crested Grebe, Snipe, Moorhen, Coot, and in the breeding season the Redshank, Mallard and Teal. In winter, Wigeon, Shoveller, Pintail, White-fronted Geese, and sometimes Bewick Swans visit some of the Forest pools.

It is on the rivers and estuaries and by the Solent shores that we have, perhaps, the greatest concentration of species, in this case mostly ducks, gulls, waders and other aquatic birds totalling nearly 60 different sorts. Some of the more interesting that have been seen at various seasons between Hurst Castle and the Beaulieu River, are Greenshank, Brent Goose, Oyster-catcher (which commenced breeding in this part of the South Coast only a few years ago), Arctic and Sandwich Terns, Grey Phalarope, Puffin, Merganser, Spotted Redshank, Spoonbill, Avocet (these last two very rarely), Gannet, Leach's Fork-tailed Petrel, Great Skua, Osprey, and Peregrine, the last-named nesting on the Isle of Wight, and at least nine species of duck.

With such a varied list of bird species resident in the New Forest, or visiting the area during the appropriate seasons, the student of ornithology need have no misgivings as to the value of the district for serious bird study. Whilst South Hampshire is not strictly on one of the busy migrational routes it is nevertheless well-sited geographically to intercept a representative variety of migrants as they proceed northwards to their nesting areas, or southwards on their return to the African continent, or in the case of winter visitors to escape the rigours of the northern winter.

The sheltered waters of the Solent provide attractions for the marine species, and luckily owing to a wider appreciation of rural amenities and conservation, there are still allowed to remain in our district, and on our coastline, areas that are still comparatively undeveloped and are therefore attractive to wildfowl and waders as places of rest and as feeding grounds.

Red-backed Shrike

Reference should be made to the loss of two species of birds that once nested in the Forest. The heronry at Vinney Ridge was abandoned some years ago, after having been established so long that the Ordnance Survey recorded its position on the maps of the district. There is, however, a much smaller heronry near Sowley, and herons often fish the Forest streams. An attempt was made in the early 1930s to re-establish Black Grouse, or Black Game, on one of the wilder heaths; eggs were obtained, hatched out under hens and the young birds turned out, but after thriving for a while, they eventually disappeared. The experiment was not repeated.

Viper

REPTILES AND AMPHIBIANS

To the student of Herpetology—the study of the Reptiles and Amphibians—the New Forest offers an interesting field, for all the native British species, namely three snakes, three lizards, two toads, the Common Frog and three newts are to be found within its perambulation. What set of conditions exists to make possible such an interesting state of affairs it is difficult to say, but the fact remains and our fauna is the richer because of it.

Of the three snakes the Adder, or Viper, is our only poisonous reptile, and because of this it must be treated with respect. It is more common in some parts of the Forest than in others and is never aggressive, seeking cover if disturbed, and seldom showing itself unless it can enjoy warm sunshine. The chief food consists of lizards, voles and mice. The Grass-snake, or Ringed snake, is perhaps less common than the Adder, and can be recognized by the yellow or white collar behind the head. It is harmless, but emits a fetid fluid when handled; the food is chiefly frogs and toads. The third, the rarest of our British snakes, is the Smooth Snake, also quite harmless; it is of a dark slate colour and has two insignificant rows of spots along its upper sides, which replace the black zigzag, and the V on the head of the Adder. The food is chiefly lizards. The Common Toad and Common Frog are well distributed, but the Natterjack Toad and the Sand Lizard are two rarities that will need all the protection that can be afforded them. The Heath Lizard, however, can be seen on the heaths in the summer on any sunny day. The third lizard, the legless, snake-like Slow-worm, may be seen in the district but it is nowhere abundant. The three newts are found in suitable ponds and pools, in some of which the spawning Common Toads and Common Frogs may be observed in early spring; in 1958 spawning of both species commenced on the exceptionally early date of 20th February.

Several streams serve to drain the New Forest, and it is possible to obtain from the Forestry Commission a fly-fisher's licence for the season, or shorter period, to catch brown trout. These fish do not grow to any great size, a half-pounder being deemed a good fish, but given a knowledge of these streams it is possible to catch several trout in a day's fishing, and to obtain opportunities to observe the wild life at the same time.

INVERTEBRATES

Crayfish, three-spined and ten-spined sticklebacks, lampreys and eels are all to be found, and sometimes one can see the large Southern Aeshna dragonfly and watch it depositing its eggs, dipping down to the surface of the water as it lays each egg, or watch the beautiful Demoiselles and Damsel-flies as they thread the sunlit reaches of the stream. For the naturalist these Forest waters are full of interest, and whilst they run very low in times of drought, and very high during spates, they contain more wild life than one might imagine.

Some rare Diptera, or Two-winged Flies, are to be found in the New Forest, and as there are said to be about 3,000 species in Britain there is ample scope in this field for the dipterist. For example, there is in this area a very rare fly whose larva lives in the droppings of the Noctule Bat, and emerges in the autumn, not an easy life-cycle to investigate. Certainly the Biting Flies (*Tabanidae*) are well represented in the New Forest district (horse-flies, clegs or stouts, etc.). The handsome stag-beetle is not uncommon, and in many places the earth-boring Minotaur beetle takes below-ground the dung of rabbit or deer in which to lay its eggs, whilst many species of wood-boring beetles, including the Long-horns, are present in numbers, besides a host of others too numerous to mention. In a few small ponds and pools, the Medicinal Leech is to be found, as is the water spider, water boatman, water snails, whirligig beetles and other species in these rather acid habitats. In suitable localities the Shorthorn grasshopper occurs, as does the Glowworm during the summer and the largest of our Wasps, the Hornet.

The Lepidoptera—the butterflies and moths—are fairly well represented here and it is said that nearly 2,000 species occur in the area, a few being extremely rare. Wide fluctuations in numbers, especially of the butterflies, may occur in successive years, but in a normal season the entomologist can expect to see in suitable habitats and on sunny days, a wide variety of species. The handsome White Admiral is on the wing in July on the outskirts of the oak-woods, where honeysuckle, the foodplant of the larva, is to be found, and the graceful, gliding flight of this butterfly between the oak-tops and the bramble blossom on which it feeds is a pleasure to see. The Silver-washed Fritillary is often abundant in the rides and open spaces, and also may be found on bramble blossom in July and August. There are two appearances of the Brimstone, one in spring when the winter hibernators emerge and lay their eggs, and the other in August, when the brood of the year are on the wing. In some years this species is abundant. In August and September the Red Admiral haunts our gardens in company with Peacocks, Small Tortoiseshells, Commas and Small Coppers, whilst on the heaths in summer, numbers of Silver-studded Blues, Small Heaths and Graylings can usually be found, and all the summer long the elf-like and attractive Speckled Wood can be seen in our deciduous woodlands, matching in its wing pattern the speckled sunlight that penetrates the leaf-canopy of the trees and shrubs. In some years the Green Hairstreak and Pearl Bordered Fritillaries are fairly numerous, but it is a pity that generally speaking two good years for butterflies seldom occur consecutively. The Glanville Fritillary is also present in certain areas.

The New Forest used to be a habitat of the Purple Emperor, but the last authentic record of this magnificient butterfly having been see here was in 1947. The Forestry Commission have very understandingly issued instructions that areas of sallow willow, the foodplant of the larva of this insect, are to be left uncut in some deciduous woodlands, as an inducement for it to return to breed.

The hawk moths are well represented, and the Pine Hawk, Hummingbird Hawk (in some years) and the Elephant Hawk are usually numerous. The day-flying 5-spot Burnet, Silver Y, Common Heath and many others occur in suitable localities and there is a considerable list of night-flying moths that are found in the Forest.

It would be well to remind readers that collecting, netting, trapping, or shooting any of the fauna of the New Forest is prohibited under the Byelaws, but application can be made to the Forestry Commission for a licence to catch insects, and to fly-fish for trout, as mentioned above.

It is hoped that the foregoing brief description of the fauna of the New Forest will give the visitor some idea of its varied character. We have within the perambulation of the Forest a wide variety of species of mammals, birds, plants, reptiles, fish, butterflies, moths and other animal life, and we must remember that such a unique heritage is ours to study and enjoy only during our lifetime, and we must in the process of that enjoyment and study ensure that we take all steps necessary to pass on to posterity every single species that we find in our midst today. Too often in the past has carelessness and selfishness robbed us for ever of a species that, given reasonable protection, might have been with us still.

Go out, then, into the woods and heaths of the New Forest, and learn from nature herself, for she has much to tell you, but remember not to destroy wild life in any form.

Red deer stag

New Forest Ponies

When the hayward drove the stock
In a herd to zome oone pleäce,
Thither vo'k begun to vlock,
Each to own his beästes feäce.

William Barnes

THE COMMONERS' ANIMALS AND THE COURT OF VERDERERS

BY D. W. YOUNG

The Commoners' animals certainly provide one of the amenities of the forest. They have also been described, not altogether unreasonably, as the architects of its scenery. It is they, more than anything else who, by their grazing, keep open the glades which are such a characteristic feature of New Forest scenery. Visitors often ask whether the animals are really wild and whether they belong to anyone. Their presence in the Forest dates back to the days of the Conqueror and possibly even before that. Up till quite recent years the ponies were the most important element of the animals turned out to graze on the Forest. Before the 1914–18 War the number of horned cattle was only a fraction of the total. They were practically confined to a few cows with their calves, turned out by Commoners who produced their own milk, and by a few men who had milk rounds. During the 1939–45 War, however, with the growing demand for milk, interest in the forest as a place for raising heifers grew, and the number of horned cattle turned out increased to four thousand, four or five times as many as the ponies. Today the position is again reversed, with 3,000 ponies and 1,900 cattle. These are typical evolutionary changes of which the whole history of the Forest is made up. The French saying "the more things change, the more they are just the same" is particularly true of the Forest. This, for instance, is not a revolutionary change but a change of emphasis. The ponies are here again, in much the same numbers as of old. The numbers of horned cattle increased temporarily to meet a national need. Let us see how it all began.

In Saxon days farming used to be carried out on what has come to be known as the open field system, which was a communal form of farming. Under the open field system the land of the manor was divided into big fields, one for the hay, another for corn and so on. In each of these fields each inhabitant had one or more strips which he cultivated, and on which he raised the appropriate crops which belonged to him. In order that he should not hinder his neighbours he was given times in which these operations should be carried out. In addition to the arable land and meadows there were commons often dedicated to different kinds of animals. The inhabitants turned their animals out on these by right. In those early days the manors often stood in a matrix of virgin and unreclaimed land, and those who thought they could get better feed that way turned out their animals there too, but it was never done by right. Some claim that the Commoners' Rights in the Forest started that way, but it is very doubtful whether any right could be so established. Indeed, with the Forest the haunt of outlaws and other undesirable characters, few would take the risk of turning animals out without protection.

After the Forest had been proclaimed a Royal Forest, the position was different. Under the forest laws, enclosures in a Royal Forest were illegal because they interfered with the free run of the deer. It would have been manifestly unfair if the king, while forbidding enclosures, took exception to people's cattle roaming on his demesne lands. Out of this fact the common rights grew. Even if they did not arise from it, they were confirmed by the declaration of the area as a Royal Forest. It should be understood, however, that these common rights did not extend to the whole year round. There were two periods when the Commoners had to keep their animals on their own ground, either by tethering or by keeping them in the byres or cow-houses. These periods were known respectively as the Winter Heyning and the Fence Month. The Winter Heyning extended from 22nd November to 4th May, a period of nearly six months, when the natural feed on the Forest was poor and the Commoners' animals would be grazing in competition with the deer. The Fence or Defence Month extended from the 20th June to 20th July. This was the period when the does were dropping their fawns, and it was

Fallow bucks

Mare and foal

Aerial view of Brockenhurst

Rounding-up ponies for the annual sales

Corsican pine in Knightwood Enclosure, beside the Bournemouth road

Aerial view of Mark Ash Wood, showing old beeches and young pines in an adjacent inclosure

desirable to leave them undisturbed. It will be seen from this that the grazing rights only extended to five months in the year. It was obviously not a very fair arrangement, because the Commoners, not being allowed to enclose their land, could not store up hay to feed the animals during these prohibited periods. Probably it is true to say that the rules about these periods were more often honoured in the breach than in the observance. To meet this difficulty the New Forest Act of 1877 includes, amongst other things, the provision that the Verderers, by making a nominal payment to the Crown of £1 each year, secure to the Commoners the right to turn out their animals all the year round.

There was another Act of Parliament which closely affected the Commoners, and that was the Deer Removal Act of 1851. This, besides doing away with the king's right to keep deer on the Forest, provided for the preparation of a register of all who had common rights in the Forest. This removed the source of much controversy and many bitter quarrels. Perhaps it would be well to make one point with regard to these common rights clear. They were attached to land and not to people; by that is meant that the Commoner exercises his right not as a personal right, but because he owns or leases land to which common rights are attached. A word too needs to be said as to the extent of these common rights. They cover all land not temporarily enclosed for forestry or agricultural purposes. This includes many roads in the Forest. The Commoners' animals have a prior right over cars in the use of such roads. This explains why ponies and cattle were once allowed to roam at large through villages like Lyndhurst, Burley and Brockenhurst, when they felt so inclined. In agricultural districts where no common rights exist, it is the liability of farmers to see that their animals are properly fenced in and do not roam in this way. In the New Forest, on the other hand, the Commoners' animals have the right to be on the open forest land, and it is up to anyone who wants to keep them off their land, to fence them out. Not all animals are commonable on the Forest. Goats, for instance, are not. Horned cattle, ponies and donkeys are. Pigs can be turned out during the pannage season, that is from the 25th September to the 22nd November; a period when acorns, beech or other mast is lying on the ground. With regard to pigs a practice has grown up, which is exercised as a privilege rather than a right, to allow breeding sows on the Forest all the year round.

It will be clear from what has been said that the animals turned out are the individual property of Commoners. How they identify their cattle is the next question which presents itself. Most Commoners know them by sight, but that would not be sufficient in the case of any dispute. Each of the Commoners has a private brand. Cows are generally taken into the cow-houses to have their calves and there is no difficulty about marking them. The hardy little ponies however are left to drop their foals in the Forest. Periodically they are rounded up and the foals are claimed by the owner of the mare with which they are running, and duly branded. Some owners, as an additional precaution, earmark their animals. It is a complicated business, this marking. The Agisters have to mark every animal which is turned out in the Forest by cutting the animal's tail. Under the Verderers' byelaws, every heifer turned out on the Forest between the ages of four months and twelve months has to be inoculated against contagious abortion, and the veterinary surgeons mark the ears of the animals so treated.

The Forestry Commissioners, who otherwise control the Forest, have little to do with the Commoners' animals except to keep them out of the Inclosures and to collect the pannage fees for pigs. The duty of regulating the exercise of common rights and looking after the Commoners' animals rests with the Verderers and their officers, the Agisters.

With the possible exception of the Coroners' Court, the Court of the Verderers is the most ancient court in the country. Its proper title is the Court of Swainmote and Attachment, though it has come to be called the Verderers' Court because the Verderers constitute it. It is one, or rather a combination of two, of the four Courts which used to administer the forest laws in all the Royal forests. These were:

1 The Court of Regard.
2 The Court of Attachment.
3 The Court of Swainmote.
4 The Justice Seat in Eyre.

The first of these Courts was not of great importance. Its function was the "lawing" of dogs, which has long ceased to be necessary. It is of interest, however, owing to the stories which have gathered round the old stirrup which hangs over the fireplace in the Verderers' Hall in the Queen's House at Lyndhurst and which figures in the Verderers' Crest. For the protection of the deer no large dogs were allowed in the Forest except mastiffs, which were allowed for personal protection against footpads and the like, provided they were "expeditated", that is, had the three front claws of their forefeet cut so that they could not chase the deer. The story attached to the stirrup is that it belonged to King Rufus, and any dog which could not pass through it had to have its claws cut off. Actually the stirrup is of early Tudor pattern and a Peke or Cairn terrier would be hard put to it, to get through.

When a man was arrested for an offence against the forest laws he had to be brought before the Court of Attachment. Its function was to record the detention and commit the defendant to the Court of Swainmote. Presumably before committing they had to be satisfied that there was a *prima facie* case against the defendant. The Court of Swainmote had to try cases sent up to them by the Court of Attachment, and other cases which had been brought direct to them. Their's was the duty to hear the evidence and find out whether the defendant was guilty or not guilty, just as a jury does. They had no power, however, to decide the punishment; that was done at the Justice Seat by the Justice-in-Eyre when he came round at intervals of three or more years. Above the place where the Verderers sit in the Verderers' Hall there is the hatchment of the Royal Arms used by the last Justice-in-Eyre ever to visit the forest. He was the Earl of Oxford, who sat in 1669, in Charles the Second's reign.

Up till the New Forest Act of 1877, by which the Verderers were reconstituted, they had nothing to do with the Commoners or their animals. They had only to administer the laws of the Forest. By that Act their number was increased from four to seven. One, the Official Verderer, was (and still is) appointed by the Queen, and six were elected by Commoners and Parliamentary Voters in the Forest. They were then given the additional duty of looking after the Commoners' rights. Under the New Forest Act of 1949, the number of Verderers was increased to ten, and certain changes were made in the method of their appointment, and in their powers and duties.

Apart from their judicial duties, the Verderers have certain important administrative duties. The general care of the Commoners' animals rests with them. Subject to the approval of the Minister of Agriculture, they have to make and amend byelaws governing the turning out of animals. They also have to judge and approve the stallions which can be turned out. By care in this direction they have done much to improve the breed of ponies. There are four officers already described as Agisters who are always on patrol. They look after the general health of the animals, trace animals that are lost, report accidents to owners and in extreme cases put animals out of their misery.

If you happen to be in the neighbourhood when the Court is sitting, it is well worth a visit. It meets at intervals of about six weeks, in January, March, May, July and November. When the clerk calls for the Court to be opened, the senior Agister stands up in the dock and with the right hand uplifted calls:

"OYEZ! OYEZ! OYEZ!

All manner of persons who have any presentment or matter or thing to do at this Court of Swainmote let him come forward and he shall be heard!

GOD SAVE THE QUEEN!"

The Court then proceeds with its duties with little formality. Anyone who feels he has a grievance can make a presentment which the Verderers discuss and adjudicate upon. Some of these presentments, and the very quaintness of the wording of the opening summons rising above the rumble and noise of lorries and cars outside, and often the whine of an aeroplane aloft, reminds one that whilst everything changes round about, the Forest still remains much the same. Deep down in the forest a man with a tractor may be skilfully extracting a massive old log from amongst its standing companions. You miss the beauty of a team of straining horses, but as you come out of the enclosures a startled foal rushes, nuzzling at its mother's belly for the only comfort it can get, just as countless thousands have done before it and as countless thousands will do in the future.

Through the Beechwoods

I must be rising and I must be going
On the roads of magic that stretch afar,
By the random rivers so finely flowing
And under the restless star.
I must be roving on the roads of glory
So I'll up and shoe me with red-deer hide
For youth must be learning the ancient story,
Let the wearied oldsters bide.

NEIL MUNRO

SIX WALKS IN THE NEW FOREST

BY P. H. CARNE

THERE are few more enjoyable ways of exploring the New Forest than to select at random one of the many possible starting-points for a ramble, and to plan one's route, with the aid of the map at the end of this Guide, as one goes along. The visitor who wishes to make the most of a brief stay may find it helpful, however, to follow a prearranged schedule. The six walks described in this article introduce something of almost every scenic aspect of the Forest. Each samples a separate area, and each is accessible at its starting and finishing points by bus or train.

(I) CADNAM TO MINSTEAD AND ASHURST (6 miles)

Cadnam, which has a good service of 'buses from Southampton, is a point where many motoring visitors gain their first glimpse of the Forest as they pass the thatched Sir John Barleycorn Inn on the Romsey-Ringwood main road. With the inn to your left and fenced Forest woodland to your right, head east along the highway-verge to the point where a gravelled track, flanked with telephone posts, diverges right. Follow this track uphill through the oaks and beeches of Rockram Wood. Festooned with holly and grazed by ponies, this wood is wholly characteristic of the type officially designated as "ancient and ornamental".

At the top of the hill you emerge on to the Cadnam-Lyndhurst road, which you follow southwards for a few yards to the first ride-gate on your right, through which you enter Shave Green Inclosure. Passing a keeper's cottage on your left, you follow a ride which strikes south-west into the heart of this planted woodland. Craggy Douglas firs make a noble avenue of your route to the first cross-rides, where you bear left through oaks and beeches to the second inclosure gate.

You enter, here, Shave Wood, an "elder sister" of Shave Green. Instead of orderly plantations, near-primeval forest scenery surrounds you as you carry on south through hoary, holly-tangled oaks and beeches. At the first track-fork, where there is a fence to your left, bear right. A few yards ahead, at another track-fork, bear left. Carry on, now, as straight ahead as a twisting trackway will allow, until you emerge past a beech-clad knoll on to the road at the northern edge of Minstead Manor.

When you join this road keep right, and at the first lane-fork bear left. At the second lane-fork, not far ahead, bear right. Hedged farmlands flank the rest of your way downhill to the Trusty Servant Inn at Minstead. Portraying an emblematic pig whose snout "not nice in diet shews", the inn-sign overlooks a 'bus-stop from which those who prefer a short walk can return to Southampton via Lyndhurst, or to Bournemouth via Ringwood.

For the second stage of this route, as indeed for most New Forest walks, stout shoes are needed. From the Trusty Servant follow the road which heads south-east to the Cadnam-Lyndhurst main road. When you join this, bear sharp left, then enter the first gate on your right to traverse Furzy Lawn Inclosure from west to east. If the going is dry, follow the track which carries on east from the gate at the far end of this mainly-coniferous wood. Emerging through scattered trees on to an open heathery "lawn", take the first path right, over slightly boggy ground, to a further tree-belt. Follow through this a well-defined track to a bridge across the winding Bartley Water.

To avoid the soggy aftermath of wet weather, you can alternatively reach the stream-bridge by bearing right beyond the eastern gate of Furzy Lawn Inclosure. Follow this woodland's fence until it bends sharply to the right, then bear left-handed, through beech and holly, to the Bartley Water's north bank, beside which a bridle path winds east to the wooden bridge.

About a hundred yards beyond the bridge, bear left through a gate into Busketts Lawn Inclosure. Flanked by lofty pines and a younger growth of oak and beech, an eastbound ride leads perfectly straight for almost a mile through this inclosure. Having crossed the second of two gravelled tracks, carry on straight ahead, and at the next ride-fork bear left. Now take the second ride on your left to cross a stile and join the Woodlands-Ashurst road. Along this bear right for about a quarter of a mile to Lyndhurst Road station, at Ashurst, and the departure-point for 'buses to Southampton. Lyndhurst and Bournemouth.

(2) LYNDHURST TO BEAULIEU (8 miles)

Frequent buses from Bournemouth and Southampton make the New Forest's "capital", Lyndhurst, a convenient centre for exploring the great woods of the middle region. From Lyndhurst High Street follow the Brockenhurst main road for half-a-mile to Goose Green. Directly opposite the entrance to the Girl Guides Association Training Centre at Foxlease, take a metalled lane which bears diagonally left past a housing estate.

Tarmac yields to gravel as you follow this lane south-east along the driftway between Park Ground and Pondhead Inclosures. Just over a mile beyond the main road another gravelled track bears right. Follow this over a cattle-grid into Parkhill Inclosure, one of the largest and most secluded planted areas of the Forest. At the first ride-junction inside this inclosure, bear left. Young conifers and older trees mingle attractively as you head east, and then south-east, along an undulating ride where the "slots" of deer are more in evidence, as a rule, than human footprints. Disregard all side turnings until, about a mile inside Parkhill Inclosure, you come to a ride-fork just beyond a valley stream-culvert. Here bear right, and cross straight over a gravelled trackway just ahead.

Carry on through conifer plantations to the next T-junction of rides, where you bear left to emerge through a gate on to a driftway between Parkhill and Stubby Copse. Bear left along this driftway, then enter the first ride-gate on your right. From a fork of rides just inside this gate bear right, and about a quarter of a mile ahead you will join another gravelled road. Follow this right-handed to a fork of gravelled tracks. From here bear left through the oaks and conifers of Denny Lodge Inclosure, a frequent haunt of buzzards and crossbills, and a quiet wood in which I have many times seen both fallow deer and roe deer.

Continue along the gravelled track across beech-fringed Woodfidley Ridge, then down to a railway level-crossing adjoined by a signal-box and cottage, Where the gravelled track veers right just beyond the railway, keep straight ahead along a ride which heads south-east through the oaks and firs of Frame Heath Inclosure. When you cross another gravelled track ignore a ride which bears half-right, and keep straight on to a further gate where you enter Frame Wood. This inexpressibly wild and lovely tract of oak and hollies is one of the haunts of the few remaining New Forest red deer.

Half a mile of winding paths precede the gate where you enter Hawkhill Inclosure, which is a stronghold of yet a fourth species of deer, the Japanese Sika. Introduced near Beaulieu in the early 1900's, Japanese deer are shy and nocturnal, and you are most likely to see them at dawn or in late evening.

Carry on south-eastwards to a gate where you emerge on to the edge of Beaulieu Heath. Ascending, you skirt the hamlet of Furzey Lodge to join a tarred lane which leads to the Brockenhurst—Beaulieu road at Hatchet Gate. Leaving Hatchet Pond and Beaulieu Heath behind you, bear left-handed to follow this road for just over a mile to Beaulieu Mill, from which there are buses to Hythe and Lymington.

(3) LYNDHURST TO BURLEY (8 miles)

From Lyndhurst follow the Brockenhurst main road south to the woodland margin at Clayhill. A gravelled lane, signposted "to High Coxlease only", here bears right. Follow this until it veers right-handed through the gate of a private dwelling. From this point carry straight on along a track flanked on the right by a woodland fence. When this fence bends right, keep straight ahead through the lovely beeches, oaks and hollies of Whitley Wood. At a track-fork (parallel with an isolated pine-grove to your right as you skirt the east edge of Butts Lawn) bear to your left, and at the next track-fork, not many yards ahead, keep to the right.

A mixture of oak, silver birch and pine flanks your route to Hursthill Inclosure's gate. This oak-wood's eastern fence lies to your right, as you carry on south along a driftway between Hursthill and New Park Plantation. Where New Park Plantation's fence bends away to your left, bear right at a T-junction of tracks to cross the tree-fringed Highland Water by a wooden bridge. Carry on, with the Highland Water to your right, to a second stream-bridge. At a cross-track directly adjoining this bear left. A few yards ahead is another track-fork where you bear right to cross the wiry grass and heather of Poundhill Heath.

On the far side of this heath you pass through a gate to follow a westerly ride through pine-wooded Poundhill Inclosure, which I well recall as a former haunt of the indigenous red squirrel. As elsewhere, the arrival of grey squirrels in the New Forest was followed by a rapid decline in numbers of the native species, and it is doubtful whether any of the red kind now survive in the district.

Emerging from Poundhill Inclosure, you climb a Douglas fir-clad slope to join the metalled Rhinefield Ornamental Drive along which you bear left. Tall exotic conifers and luxuriant rhododendrons flank your route to a forester's cottage, directly beyond which you enter a ride-gate on your right. Heading west through the mingling conifers, oaks and beeches of Rhinefield Sandys Inclosure, you pass through another inclosure gate to cross the main Lyndhurst-Bournemouth road.

Beyond a further gate, straight ahead, you follow a ridge-top ride through Burley Old Inclosure. A stronghold of badgers and fallow deer, this wood is notable for the beauty of its ancient oaks and beeches. Long, shade-dappled vistas spread away on either hand as you head westwards to the gateway bordering Burley New Inclosure. Pass through this and continue along a conifer-bordered ride which presently joins a gravelled track. Follow this track north-westwards until it bends right, then follow a grass ride straight ahead to emerge through a gate on to the Lyndhurst-Burley road. Follow this road leftwards to the Queen's Head Inn at Burley, from which there are 'buses to Southampton, Ringwood and Bournemouth.

(3a) BROCKENHURST TO BURLEY (7 miles)

As an alternative to starting from Lyndhurst, you may begin the walk described above from Brockenhurst, which is more easily accessible than almost any other New Forest walking-centre.

Leave Brockenhurst station by the exit on the "up" side, and follow the station-approach road to the main-road level-crossing. Here bear left, then, almost immediately, left again, through Brockenhurst village. Having crossed the Sway road, carry straight on to a "watersplash" ford adjoined by a footbridge, directly beyond which bear right-handed at a T-junction of roads. At the next T-junction, where Meerut-road joins the road to Rhinefield, a well-defined footpath strikes north-west, away from the tarmac and into the Forest.

Following this, you cross the grass and gorse of Butts Lawn and Black Knowl and join a gravelled forest track along which you bear right over Bolderford Bridge. Beyond this bridge bear left, with the Highland Water to your left and the fence of oak-wooded New Park Plantation to your right. Presently this fence bends right, but you carry on straight ahead to cross the tree-fringed Highland Water by another rustic bridge. At this point you join Route 3, described above, and continue along it towards Burley.

(4) BROCKENHURST TO BURLEY (9 miles)

A stopping-place for most of the main-line trains between London and Bournemouth, Brockenhurst is also a junction for a branch serving Lymington and there are frequent buses from Southampton, Lyndhurst, Lymington and Bournemouth.

Leaving Brockenhurst station by the exit on the "up" (or north) side bear sharp left. Cross a railway footbridge, then bear left along a tarred road beside the railway. Where this road becomes a footpath, cross a stile on your right-hand side and follow a tree-lined path to the Brockenhurst-Sway road. Along this bear left to Brockenhurst School, directly beyond which bear right-handed to follow a gravel-surface path over grassy common land to the Burley road.

Bear left along this to Brockenhurst Weirs, where farmland on your left veers away from the road. Follow the road for a further hundred yards to a stream-culvert, having crossed which bear left, with the stream to your left, to follow a rising moorland path in a south-westerly direction.

An undulating, pine-besprinkled heath-scape spreads about you as you cross a tarmac road and ford a stream, beyond which your footpath mounts a second moorland knoll. At a track-fork on the top of this, bear left and carry on parallel with a line of telephone posts to a gravelled lane, along which you bear right. Take the first path bearing diagonally left through self-sown pines to join another gravelled lane, along which bear left to leave the Hincheslea Woods behind you.

Having crossed a bog-causeway and the line of an old railway, this gravelled lane climbs steeply to the crest of a heathery ridge from which extensive moorland views may be enjoyed in all directions. At the ridge-top track-junction bear right to join the Lymington-Burley road. Follow this right to the first road-junction and here bear left to follow a wood-edge path to the first gate on your right, where you enter Set Thorns Inclosure. Following a sandy track through conifers and oaks, carry straight on over the first cross-rides to a junction of five rides, where you bear half-left and head downhill. Soon emerging through a gate, bear to your left at a junction of tracks to cross again the old railway, beyond which a valley path strikes north-westwards to a metalled moorland lane.

Cross this, and pass through a gateway into Wilverley Inclosure, where dark-crowned conifers line your route as you head west along a gravelled track to the Lyndhurst-Bournemouth road. When you join this bear left to the old Holmsley station.

Beyond the old railway-bridge take the first track on your right to an old mill. On the near side of this bear right to follow a well-made gravelled path along the edge of Holmsley Bog as far as the second inclosure gateway on your left. Inside this follow a ride which veers right-handed through Holmsley Inclosure, climbing steadily to a further gate which leads out on to the moors beyond Holmsley Lodge. Cross a tarmac road and follow a track to the end of the lodge paddocks, where at a fork of tracks bear right and descend to a rustic railway-bridge. Cross this, then follow the moorland track ahead, downhill, then up to another track-fork, where you bear right to rejoin the Lymington-Burley road on the edge of Burley. Follow this left-handed, downhill through trees, to the Queen's Head Inn.

(5) PICKET POST TO MINSTEAD (8 miles)

Picket Post, near the Forest's verge three miles towards Cadnam from Ringwood, can be reached by 'bus from Southampton, Lyndhurst, Ringwood and Bournemouth. Alight at the Burley turning and follow the left-hand of two tracks intersecting the angle between the Cadnam and Burley roads. Heading east, this crosses the moors to Ridley Wood, which is so enchantingly secluded that one can well believe reports that it was once a smugglers' hideout. Gnarled oaks and pollard beeches flank the hollow "Smugglers' Lane" to a fork of tracks near the eastern exit from the wood, where you bear left to follow a causeway-path over a holly-bordered bog.

At a cross-tracks on the ridge ahead, bear left to skirt a beech-clump and ascend to a further track-fork, where you veer right. On the western verge of Berry Beeches you join a well-defined ridge-tip track; along this bear left, then almost immediately turn right to follow a track which heads north-east towards Old House, where you join a gravelled forest track. Following this right-handed, head downhill through oak plantations to a T-junction of gravelled tracks, where you bear left. Heading again north-east, you traverse the great inclosure of Oakley, where buzzards and foxes, fallow and roe deer have their home.

After crossing a ridge which commands wide vistas over the tree-tops all around, carry on downhill to a crossing of tracks where you bear right to cross Bratley Water by a rail-and-log footbridge. Lying a little to the left of a ride-ford, this is approached by a narrow path through a dim conifer plantation. Having crossed the stream, rejoin the parallel ride, which rises steadily to a gateway where you enter Mark Ash Wood. Beyond this gate keep straight ahead to a track-fork at the head of a boggy vale. Bear left here, and at the next track-fork bear right to skirt left-handed of a post-and-rail-fenced hillside inclosure-in-miniature.

On the ridge-top in the centre of this beautiful old beech wood cross straight over a gravelled road and follow a track which joins the Emery Down-Ringwood road on Wooson's Hill. Along this road bear right to the first gateway on your left. Entering this, you follow a ride downhill to the Highland Water. Having crossed this by a footbridge, carry on through the dense plantations of Holmhill Inclosure to another ride-gate. Continuing north-east alongside the fence of Highland Water Inclosure, you soon emerge on to a gravelled forest track. Along this bear right, past Robinsbush Farm, to a junction of roads from which you follow the Minstead signpost, straight ahead, to the "Trusty Servant", close to a bus route to Southampton.

(6) NOMANSLAND TO PICKET POST (11 miles)

The first $2\frac{1}{2}$ miles of this walk through the wild and hilly north-western Forest can be omitted by starting from Telegraph Post, which is served by occasional buses between Southampton and Fordingbridge. Nomansland is the terminal point of a 'bus-service from Southampton, and also has 'bus connections with Salisbury.

From the Lamb Inn at Nomansland follow the Fritham road south-west for half a mile to the point where bordering woods give way to rising moorland. Here, where the road veers left, keep straight ahead along a gravelled heathland track, which gives place to grass as you pass a Forest keeper's cottage on your right. With Franchises Wood and the Wiltshire border to your right, carry on downhill into wild and lovely Crow's Nest Bottom, where you cross a stream-culvert. From here an ill-defined footpath strikes diagonally uphill to emerge through trees on to the Cadnam-Fordingbridge road. Follow this road right-handed to the hilltop signpost at Telegraph Post, then take a level gravelled track which strikes half-left across the heath. From a track-fork on the tree-verge, bear left to a gate where you enter Islands Thorns Inclosure.

At the first ride-fork inside this placid oak and beech wood, bear right-handed. Ignore the next right-forking ride and carry on steadily downhill to a ride T-junction. Bear right here, and right again at the next ride-junction. Cross Latchmore Brook, then immediately bear left to follow a ride which runs closely parallel with this stream for more than a mile. Apart from the prattling of water and the periodic wing-claps of wood-pigeons in the treetops, on a still day there is scarcely a sound or a movement in these woods, unless you are lucky enough to chance upon a herd of fallow deer.

Carry on without a turn until you join a gravelled forest track just west of Fritham Bridge. Follow this track right-handed between two inclosure fences, and at the point where it bends sharp right pass through a gateway, straight ahead, to enter Amberwood Inclosure. Follow a south-westerly ride through this quiet valley oak wood, and at the second cross-rides bear left to cross Latchmore Brook by a plank-bridge. Pass through two gates, then carry on south through Sloden Inclosure, ignoring all turnings right and left as you ascend to a further gate. Here, where you enter Old Sloden Wood, face half-right to follow a downhill track through brackeny glades and yew groves. Soon you join a gravelled track, along which you bear right across the moors into the Dockens Water valley. After skirting right of Holly Hatch Cottage, your gravelled track veers left through a gate into oak-wooded Broomy Inclosure.

Carry on through this wood until the gravel track is joined by a path from the left. Another path, half-hidden in summer by bracken, here bears right. Follow this past the point where another path joins it from the left, and at the next ride-fork bear left, through conifer-groves, to a further gate. Cross the ride directly beyond this to follow a rising path through the oak and holly of High Corner Wood. Cross a gravelled track at right-angles to your own to follow another over heathland commanding magnificent views of the hilly moors and woodlands to the west.

When you join a tarmac road bear right, with Milkham Inclosure at first on your left, and then old woods on either hand. Where a gravelled track bears sharp left towards Roe Cottage, you bear half left to follow a ridge-top ride towards Appleslade Inclosure. With the fence of this shady conifer plantation to your right and the hillside oaks of Red Shoot Wood to your left, carry on south-west along a track which soon emerges on to lofty, open moorland. Joining a gravelled road, you follow the fence of Great Linford Inclosure to Linford hamlet, where you cross a stream of the same name. Where the road, now metalled, takes its second right-hand bend beyond Linford Brook, carry on straight ahead to follow a rising moorland track to Picket Post, where you end your walk at the 'bus-stop on the Cadnam-Ringwood road.

MOTORING WITHOUT MAPS IN THE NEW FOREST

Two holiday day-tours planned by PETER and PATRICIA LEWIS

MAP-READING isn't everyone's forte, so these routes are planned to be read out by a passenger to the driver as you go along, and direct you by such easily-identified landmarks as telephone kiosks, inn names, bus stops, etc., as well as sign-posts. The routes are planned in close co-operation with the Automobile Association and are derived from the type of route card issued to A.A. members on tour. To find the prettiest scenery, we often leave the main roads and follow narrow, winding byways.

The rear endpaper map shows the routes in outline.

Just master the simple abbreviations below and you will be able to read out the route, stage by stage, to the driver. Directions are not given when the way ahead is obviously straightforward and therefore not all road junctions you pass are mentioned. Mileages, showing the distance between key points, are printed at the side of the route.

ABBREVIATIONS AND SYMBOLS

asc. *ascend, ascent*	m. *mile*	sta. *station*
br. *bridge*	NT *National Trust*	t., tng. *turn, turning*
ch. *church*	rly. *railway*	T-rd. *T-junction*
desc. *descend, descent*	R. *river*	Tele. kiosk { *G.P.O. telephone box*
fwd. *forward*	rd. *road*	
immed. *immediately*	rt. *right*	unclass. *unclassified road*
LC. *level crossing*	S.P. *signpost*	X-ways } *cross roads*
lt. *left*	st. *street*	X-rds.

LYNDHURST AND THE NEW FOREST

Both routes start and end at Lyndhurst, within easy reach of such towns as Bournemouth, Salisbury, Winchester and Southampton.

We loved every minute we spent motoring over these roads in the largest and oldest of Britain's open forests—the woodland glades, the aristocratic deer, flowers that produced a sudden blaze of colour, the tough, intelligent ponies and noisy piglets who eat the acorns. We found no difficulty in obtaining good midday snacks at reasonable prices. There is an abundance of picnic spots, too.

Children will prefer the second route, which includes the Motor Museum at Beaulieu, and Buckler's Hard, where British men-o-war were built in Nelson's day. There are one-hour cruises on Beaulieu River.

A warning note—please don't stop and encourage the ponies towards the road, for this is how many ponies have been injured in recent years.

ABOUT ROUTE I

Distance $25\frac{3}{4}$ *miles*

This tour starts from the friendly little town of Lyndhurst, with its fascinating curio and antique shops, and runs northwards beside the golf course before turning off to Minstead with its typical village green and quaint inn sign at The Trusty Servant. Spare a few minutes for the short diversion to Furzey Gardens, at their best in May but always peaceful and luxuriant, before continuing to Rufus Stone. The memorial, at the foot of a lovely descent with widespread views of wooded country, has inscriptions on three sides that tell how William Rufus was slain by an arrow 869 years ago. (see page 9).

From Rufus Stone a fairly rapid main road section is followed by a wide sweep into open country that eventually brings us back to the main road again, and a three-mile run to Picket Post. Here the route turns southwards to Burley Street and continues—through charming wooded country—to Burley with its fascinating Queen's Head Inn where there is a wishing well, and where mine host has a remarkable collection of weapons, antiques and horse brasses, and a fund of stories about the old smuggling days. This famous New Forest inn is conveniently situated for a mid-day halt.

From Burley it is a lovely run through the heart of the forest for almost ten miles to Lyndhurst, via the venerable Knightwood Oak, of tremendous girth, Mark Ash Wood, Bolderwood Grounds, and a charming group of thatched cottages opposite the Swan Inn where the route rejoins the main road.

Our running time, in light traffic and without stops, was 3 hours.

OPEN TO VIEW

(*Information correct at the time of going to Press*)

FURZEY, MINSTEAD. Open daily March to October inclusive, 10 a.m. to dusk. Collecting box for the National Gardens Scheme for Retired District Nurses Benefit Fund, and the National Trust's Gardens Scheme.

READER—ROUTE 1

LYNDHURST

From Free Car Park t.rt. into High Street and follow the one-way system right-handed round the town, back to the High Street. Just after passing the church, t.lt. into Romsey Rd. singposted "Romsey" (A.337). In 1½m. t.lt. *unclass.* (S.P. Minstead, Stoney Cross).

2½ Minstead (The Trusty Servant). Fwd. passing tele. kiosk on rt. In ¼m. t.lt. at Minstead Village Hall and bus stop. Bear rt. at Green and shortly fork lt. for

¾ Furzey Gardens. Return by same road to Minstead Hall. T.lt. and follow direction Ringwood. In ½m. t.lt. at T-rd. and cattle grid on to dual carriageway (A.31). Take next tng. rt., off dual carriageway, (S.P. Rufus Stone, Cadnam), and immed. lt. (S.P. Rufus Stone, Brook, Bramshaw). Desc. to

1¼ Rufus Stone (on lt.). Return by same road to dual carriageway and t.lt. Then t.rt. so as to proceed in the reverse direction along the dual carriageway. (S.P. Minstead, Ringwood, Lyndhurst). Follow A.31 west.

1 Stoney Cross (Compton Arms Hotel). In ½m. at Stoney Cross X-rds. t.rt. *unclass.* (S.P. Fritham, Fordingbridge) passing disused aerodrome on lt. In 1m. t.lt. (S.P. Linwood, Moyles Court). In 2½m. t.lt. at T-rd. (S.P. Cadnam, Ringwood). In 1m. farther at next T-rd. t.rt. on to main road (S.P. Bournemouth).

7¾ Picket Post (A.A. Box 794). (*Joining point for readers from Shaftesbury, Dorchester, Wimborne, Bournemouth and Ringwood*). T.lt. *unclass.* (S.P. Burley) and in 1¼m. bear lt. (S.P. Burley, Brockenhurst).

1½ Burley Street. Keep rt. (S.P. Brockenhurst).

1¼ Burley (War Memorial). T.lt. then keep lt. at Queen's Head (S.P. Lyndhurst, Southampton). Follow direction Lyndhurst, Southampton. In ¾m. keep rt. (S.P. Lyndhurst, Southampton) and in ¼m. keep lt. (S.P. Lyndhurst).

3½ Junction of *unclass.* road with Lyndhurst Road. Keep lt. on to Lyndhurst Road (S.P. Lyndhurst) and in ¼m. t.lt. *unclass.* and cross cattle grid. (In 200 yds. a short walk to the right leads to Knightwood Oak). Fwd. and in 1m. cross cattle grid into Mark Ash Wood. In 1m. cross another cattle grid.

2½ Bolderwood Grounds (Entrance to Bolderwood Lodge on left, immediately after crossing cattle grid). T.rt. at cattle grid and follow track for 200 yds. to a road where t.rt. and desc.

2¾ New Forest Inn. Keep rt. and at top of asc. keep rt. at ch., passing entrance to Northerwood House on lt. In ½m. at The Swan Inn t.lt. on to main rd. (A.35) for

1 LYNDHURST

New-born Roe deer fawn, photographed in Holmsley Inclosure

Sand lizard on tree stump

The Queen's House, Lyndhurst

Pollard beeches in Knightwood Inclosure

Grey squirrel poised on a tree-trunk

Fox cubs awaiting food brought by their parents

ABOUT ROUTE 2

Distance $24\frac{3}{4}$ miles without diversions but including Ornamental Drive

The route runs southwards from Lyndhurst—with a cricket pitch in a delightful setting on the left soon after leaving the High Street—to Beaulieu Road with its pretty group of fir trees opposite the hotel. There are facilities at the hotel for horse and pony trekking.

From the hotel (prices for a snack lunch we found very reasonable) the route strikes eastwards across rolling heathland to a busy road that runs into Dibden Purlieu, and then southwards across the expanse of Beaulieu Heath to Hill Top. Try and find time for the 5-mile diversion to Exbury Gardens, a riot of colour from Easter to Whitsun when the rhododendrons and azaleas are in full bloom—200 acres and magnificently impressive.

From Hill Top it is little more than a mile to Beaulieu with its attractive main street, and Lord Montagu's Palace House and Abbey in their charming setting on the banks of the Beaulieu River. Also here is the famous Montagu Motor Museum of veteran and vintage cars, and the Motor Cycle Museum with machines dating from 1899. Allow at least two hours in Beaulieu, for one should not miss the impressive Palace House, or the ruins of the Abbey, founded by King John in 1204. There is a fine beamed restaurant, and a cafeteria with good service and reasonable prices.

From Beaulieu there is a diversion of five miles to Buckler's Hard, an age-old riverside hamlet where some of Nelson's men-o-war were built with oak from the New Forest, including his favourite ship, the *Agamemnon*, in 1781. The Maritime Museum—opened in 1963 by Lord Mountbatten—recaptures the spirit of those stirring days.

From Hatchet Pond it is a very pretty run through the woods of Stockley Inclosure, where there are countless picnic spots, and beyond to Brockenhurst which is approached across a river bridge. From here we have given two routes back to Lyndhurst—a short one via the main road if time is pressing, or a more leisurely one through the woods and along the superb Ornamental Drive.

Our running time, in light traffic and without stops, was 4 hours and included the Exbury Gardens and Buckler's Hard diversions and the Rhododendron Drive from Brockenhurst to Lyndhurst.

OPEN TO VIEW (*Information correct at the time of going to Press*).

EXBURY GARDENS. Open from Easter to Whitsun, every Sunday and Wednesday, from 2 p.m. to 7 p.m. Admission charge. MONTAGU MOTOR MUSEUM, PALACE HOUSE AND GARDENS, BEAULIEU ABBEY. Daily throughout the year, except Christmas Day: April—October: 10.30 a.m. to 6 p.m. (Abbey 10 a.m. to 7 p.m.).

November—March: 10 a.m. to 5 p.m. except Palace House (Sundays only). Abbey: 10 a.m. to dusk. Admission charges for Museum, Palace House and Gardens 3s. Chd. 1s. 6d. Abbey 1s. Chd. 6d. Car Park free. BUCKLER'S HARD MARITIME MUSEUM, April—October: Open daily 10.30 a.m. to 6 p.m. November—March: Saturdays and Sundays only, 10 a.m. to 5 p.m. Admission charges.

READER—ROUTE 2

LYNDHURST

From Free Car Park t.rt. into High St. Leave by B3056 (S.P. Beaulieu).

3½ Beaulieu Road Station. Cross rly. br. and pass Beaulieu Road Hotel. Then in ¼m. branch lt. *unclass.* (S.P. Hythe). In 2½m. fwd. at SLOW sign and X-rds. (S.P. Hythe, Fawley). Then in ¾m. at T-rd. and SLOW sign t.rt.

4½ Dibden Purlieu (The Heath Hotel). At X-rds. t.rt. B3054 (S.P. Beaulieu) and cross Beaulieu Heath.

2 Hill Top (Royal Oak Inn). (*See footnote 1 for optional diversion to Exbury Gardens.*) Keep rt. B3054 (Beaulieu, Brockenhurst, Lymington). In 1m. pass entrance to Beaulieu Abbey (on rt.). Then cross R. br. into

1¼ Beaulieu. (*See footnote 2 for optional diversion to Buckler's Hard.*) Keep fwd. B3054 (S.P. Lymington). Follow direction Lymington. In 1¼m. bear rt. (S.P. Brockenhurst) passing

1¼ Hatchet Pond (on lt.). In 4m. branch lt. (B3055) and cross R. br. into

5 Brockenhurst. (*See footnote 3 for direct route back to Lyndhurst.*) (Joining Point at railway station and level crossing for readers from Bournemouth and Lymington.) At T-rd. t.rt. (A337. Lyndhurst). Continue over L.C. and immed. t.lt. into Brookley Rd. In ¼m. over X-rds. (S.P. Rhinefield) and shortly pass through shopping area and water splash. Then at T-rd. t.rt. and follow direction Rhinefield Rd.

3¼ Rhinefield Lodge (on lt.). T.rt. and shortly pass through gate and over br. Continue through Ornamental Drive. In 1½m. on reaching main road at cattle grid t.rt. In another 2m. at Swan Inn keep rt. into

4 LYNDHURST

Footnote 1. *Diversion to Exbury Gardens—5 miles extra.*

Hill top (Royal Oak Inn). Take second tng. to the lt. *unclass.* (S.P. Exbury, Lepe) leaving inn on the rt. In ¾m. pass through gate.

2½ Exbury Gardens (entrance on rt.). Return by same road to

2½ Hill top (Royal Oak Inn). At T-rd. t.lt. B3054 (S.P. Beaulieu, Brockenhurst, Lymington).

Footnote 2. *Diversion to Buckler's Hard—4½ miles extra.*
Beaulieu. Keep fwd. B3054 (S.P. Lymington). Then in ¼m. branch lt. *unclass.* (S.P. Buckler's Hard). In another ½m. branch lt. *unclass.* (S.P. Buckler's Hard) and in another 1¼m. keep lt. In ½m. enter

2½ Buckler's Hard (Car Park). Return for 2¼m. to rd-junc. by same route and turn sharp lt. (S.P. Brockenhurst, Lymington). In 1m. bear rt. (S.P. Brockenhurst) passing

3¼ Hatchet Pond (on lt.).

Footnote 3. *Direct route from Brockenhurst to Lyndhurst*—saving 3¼m. Brockenhurst. At T-rd. t.rt. A337 (Lyndhurst) and continue over L.C. Then fwd. passing the Railway Inn on rt. Follow direction Lyndhurst. In 3½m bear lt. at Goose Green (A35. Southampton). Then t.lt. (signposted Southampton) and half-way down the High Street turn rt. for car park.

4 LYNDHURST

PLACES TO JOIN THE ROUTES

Route No. 1. From Shaftesbury, Dorchester, Wimborne, Bournemouth and Ringwood join at Picket Post on the A31 road from Ringwood to Cadnam. From other directions join at the Lyndhurst starting point—the Free Car Park in the High Street.

Route No. 2. From Bournemouth and Lymington join at Brockenhurst Railway Station and Level Crossing. From other directions join at the Lyndhurst starting point.

Both routes. From London, Winchester, Newbury, Salisbury, Portsmouth and Southampton join at the Lyndhurst starting point.

Heron

Woodpecker

This is the weather the cuckoo likes
And so do I;
When showers betumble the chestnut spikes
And nestlings fly:
And the little brown nightingale bills his best,
And they sit outside "The Travellers' Rest,"
And maids come forth sprig-muslin drest,
And citizens dream of the south and west,
And so do I!

THOMAS HARDY

GENERAL INFORMATION

HOW TO REACH THE FOREST

THE New Forest is traversed by the main Southern Region line from London (Waterloo) to Bournemouth, and enjoys a frequent service of fast trains. Most expresses stop at Southampton and also at Brockenhurst, from which points local trains may be taken to other stations in or near the Forest. The journey from London takes a little under two hours. Rail connections with other parts of England may be made through either Bournemouth or Southampton.

For more local transport, the south and west of the Forest is well served by rail. The stations at Lyndhurst Road (two miles from Lyndhurst), Beaulieu Road (four miles from Beaulieu), Brockenhurst and Sway, are all convenient starting points for rambles across the Forest heaths, whilst Hinton Admiral, New Milton, and Lymington stations are only a few miles from the Forest boundaries.

The north-western portions of the Forest, however, are not crossed or touched upon by any railway line, the nearest station being at Salisbury.

ACCESS BY FERRY

Hythe, on the eastern fringe of the Forest, is linked to Southampton by a half-hourly ferry service, the crossing taking about fifteen minutes. This provides a quick and pleasant approach to the Forest for pedestrians and cyclists. There is also a fairly frequent ferry service (for cars as well as pedestrians) to Lymington from the Isle of Wight.

MOTOR BUSES

The principal company operating motor buses in the New Forest is the Hants and Dorset Motor Services, Ltd., of The Square, Bournemouth, (Bournemouth 23371) from whom timetables (price 10p, postage 7p.) may be obtained. Many of the New Forest routes begin at the Civic Centre, Southampton, within a few minutes' walk of the Central Station. The Bournemouth routes begin at the Omnibus Station in the Square, Bournemouth.

The Wilts and Dorset Motor Services Ltd., of 8, Endless Street, Salisbury (Salisbury 6855) operate services close to the north of the New Forest, with connections to points in Wiltshire. (Timetables price 10p, postage 5p).

Despite a large number of services, there still remain several extensive "busless areas" within the Forest. It is, in fact, easier to reach many parts of the Forest by bus from Bournemouth or Southampton, than to travel around them from the villages within the Forest borders. This is not to suggest that the visitor will not find many of the services of great help to him; but rather that he should plan his route carefully with the aid of a map and a timetable.

EXPRESS COACH SERVICES

The New Forest is served by the Royal Blue Express Services from London to Bournemouth and the West of England, which stop at Southampton, Totton, Lyndhurst, Brockenhurst, New Milton, Highcliffe, and Christchurch; certain routes also serve Lymington, Romsey and Ringwood. (Timetables 5p).

Messrs. Associated Motorways operate through services from Bournemouth, Salisbury and Southampton to many towns in the Midlands and South Wales. (Timetables free).

Particulars of all these services may be obtained from:

Hants and Dorset Coach Station, Bedford Place, Southampton (Southampton 32240).

MOTORING

The main roads across the Forest are well-surfaced and clearly signposted, and are provided with drawing-in places at intervals for those who wish to halt awhile and enjoy the scenery. There are also many attractive side-roads.

The parking of cars in the forest after dark, except as authorised by the Camping regulations (see below), is an offence against the byelaws.

RIDING

The New Forest, with its wide expanses of unenclosed common land and shady woodland tracks, is ideal country for the horseman. Generally speaking, there are no restrictions on riding across the open heaths or along any of the forest rides, but particular care should be taken to see that all Inclosure gates are closed after passing through. There are riding schools, where horses may be hired, at most of the Forest villages.

Camping on the Open Forest

CAMPING

The Forestry Commission has two equipped camps, and also permits camping on a number of informal camping areas with only a minimum of facilities. A map showing the situation of these is obtainable on request from the Forestry Commission, Queen's House, High Street, Lyndhurst, Hants. SO4 7NH. (Phone: Lyndhurst 2801)

CHARGES (1972)

20p per person per night

10p per night for 5-15 year olds

Children under 5 years free of charge

Schools and approved Youth Organisations 5p per head per night by arrangement (informal areas only)

Charges are subject to revision from time to time, and are also subject to a 10% increase for Value Added Tax.

PERMITS

New arrivals at the equipped camps should book in at the Warden's Office, whilst those intending to camp in one of the informal areas should obtain a permit from one of the camping offices; the office in Lyndhurst Car Park off the High Street is open daily from 9.00 am. until dusk; the others (see map) are open at weekends during the height of the season. No advance bookings can be accepted.

Permits for the equipped sites and the informal areas are not interchangeable.

A limited number of seasonal permits is issued for the equipped camps only—details on application. Sub-letting is not permitted.

Residential caravans, lorries and trade vehicles are not allowed on the Forest.

Members of the public are permitted to enter Forestry Commission land and buildings entirely at their own risk on the condition that they will have no claim whatsoever against the Forestry Commission for any loss, damage or injury howsoever caused.

SEASON

The camping season runs from the Thursday before Good Friday or April 1st whichever is the earlier, until the last weekend before or including 1st. October. Holmsley camp remains open until the end of October.

THE EQUIPPED CAMPS

HOLMSLEY CAMP

Holmsley Old Aerodrome, Hinton, Christchurch, Hampshire.

Open site on the Lyndhurst-Christchurch Road (A35) some 8 miles southwest of Lyndhurst on the edge of the Forest.

Toilet blocks, wash basins, razor points, hot and cold water and showers, chemical disposal points.

Hard standing for caravans and vehicles.

Shops cater for everyday needs; bottled gas and mantles are stocked by the Warden. Small Cafe on site.

The main entrance closes about 11.00 pm, but there is a "Late Arrivals Park".

HOLLANDS WOOD CAMP

Brockenhurst, Hampshire.

Woodland site on the Lyndhurst-Brockenhurst Road (A337) some 3½ miles south of Lyndhurst, in the heart of the Forest.

Toilet blocks, wash basins, razor points, hot and cold water and showers, chemical disposal points.

Warden stocks bottled gas and mantles; milkman calls daily. Brockenhurst shops within easy reach.

The main entrance closes about 11.00 pm. but there is a "Late Arrivals Park".

THE INFORMAL CAMPING AREAS

There is a choice of open or wooded areas, some with chemical disposal points and water, others with no facilities. They are shown on the map and are signposted. Campers in these areas may not use the facilities on the equipped camp sites.

It is recommended that you bring a chemical toilet. Failing that dig a latrine at least two feet deep, keep it disinfected and fill it in at the end of your stay with at least one foot of cover. Foul water must be treated in the same way.

Additional water supplies and village toilets are shown on map.

YOUTH HOSTELS

The Norleywood hostel is in the south-east, close to the hamlet of Norleywood, which lies three miles north-east of Lymington and four miles south-west of Beaulieu, about a mile to the east of the main road joining those two places.

The Burley hostel is on the south-eastern side of Burley village, in the south-west of the Forest. It lies just north of the road from Burley to Brockenhurst.

The Southampton hostel is also a convenient centre for reaching the New Forest, seven miles distant by road, and there is another hostel at Winchester. For details see the Handbook of the Youth Hostels Association, obtainable 5p (postage 2½p) from the Secretary, 8, St. Stephen's Hill, St. Albans, Herts.

HOTEL ACCOMMODATION

This is ample and good. Hotels within the Forest Boundary include the following:

At Lyndhurst: Crown Hotel, Evergreens, Forest Lodge, Ormonde House, Parkhill Hotel, Stag Hotel, Forest Point Hotel, Lyndhurst Park Hotel.

At Ashurst:	New Forest Hotel.
At or near Cadnam:	Furnival Hotel, Compton Arms (Stoney Cross).
At Minstead:	Ye Olde Trusty Servante Inn.
At Brockenhurst:	Balmer Lawn Hotel, Cloud Hotel, Forest Park Hotel, Rose & Crown, Watersplash, Whitley Ridge, Brockenhurst Hotel, Fernbank Guest House.
At Burley:	Burley Manor Hotel, Moorhill Hotel.
At or near Beaulieu:	Montagu Arms, Beaulieu Road Hotel.
At Linwood, near Ringwood:	Red Shoot Inn.
At Godshill:	The Fighting Cocks.
At Bramshaw:	Bramble Hill Hotel.
At Sway:	Pine Trees Hotel.

Besides these, there are others, too numerous for mention here, at Southampton, Hythe, Lymington, Milford-on-Sea, Barton-on-Sea, New Milton, Highcliffe, Christchurch, Bournemouth, Ferndown, Ringwood, Fordingbridge, Salisbury and Romsey, all within easy daily travelling distance of the New Forest.

FIELD SPORTS

A limited number of permits for fishing in the Forest is issued each year. Further information may be obtained from the Deputy Surveyor, The Queen's House, Lyndhurst.

The New Forest district has its own packs of foxhounds, buckhounds, and beagles; and otterhounds occasionally visit the area.

There is a bathing beach at Lepe, on the Solent, and the sea lies only a few miles beyond the Forest boundary at the resorts of Highcliffe, Barton and Milford-on-Sea. Lymington has open-air seawater baths, and is also a yachting centre.

There are golf clubs at Lyndhurst, Burley, Brockenhurst and Bramshaw.

THE PROTECTION OF WILD LIFE

Under the New Forest Byelaws, all wild life within the Forest is protected, and one may not dig up any plants, nor hunt, trap, or shoot any animal or bird, without the written consent of the Forestry Commission. These restrictions apply also to fishing, the taking of birds' eggs, and "sugaring" in order to catch insects. Anyone desiring to make collections for scientific purposes should approach the Deputy Surveyor to ascertain whether permission may be granted.

A NOTE ON MAPS

The most useful map for the visitor is the Ordnance Survey Tourist Map entitled "New Forest", 50p from H.M.S.O., etc. One-inch sheets Nos. 179, "Bournemouth" for areas west of Lyndhurst, and 180, "The Solent", for Lyndhurst and the eastern parts of the Forest, also cover the district. Each is priced at 40p.

NOTABLE TREES

There are two arboreta or collections of rare trees open to the public in the New Forest, namely, the Bolderwood Arboretum beside the main road from Lyndhurst, via Emery Down, to Ringwood, and the Ornamental Drive near Rhinefield Lodge, west of Brockenhurst. A note of routes to the collections appears on p.93. The finest trees in each collection have been measured by Mr. A. F. Mitchell, of the Forestry Commission Research Branch, who has supplied the information on which the following lists are based. They give first the scientific name of each tree, then the English name and country of origin, then the height in feet, and finally the girth in feet and inches, measured at the customary "breast height" of 4 feet 3 inches above ground level. These specimen trees were planted about 1860, so they are now about 110 years old. Labels will be found at the foot of most of the trees.

In 1960 a new arboretum was started, within a deer ring fence, on the west side of the ornamental drive.

BOLDERWOOD ARBORETUM

Abies procera	Noble silver fir, Oregon, U.S.A.	128′ x 13′ 5″
Araucaria araucana	Monkey puzzle, Chile	67′ x 6′ 5″
Cedrus deodara	Deodar cedar, Himalayas	105′ x 8′ 6½″
Cryptomeria japonica	Japanese cedar	93′ x 8′ 8″
Picea sitchensis	Sitka spruce, Alaska	137′ x 12′ 9″
Pinus griffithii	Himalayan pine	103′ x 10′ 9″
Pinus montezumae var. hartwegii	Mexican pine	75′ x 6′ 7″
Pinus pinaster	Maritime pine, Portugal	100′ x 7′ 7″
Pinus strobus	Weymouth pine, Eastern United States	113′ tall
Pinus rigida	Pitch pine, Eastern United States (Tallest recorded in Britain)	64′ x 7′ 6″
Pinus nigra var. maritima	Corsican pine	120′ x 7′ 7″

Pinus nigra var. caramanica	Crimean pine	130′ x 11′ 11″
Pinus radiata	Monterey pine, California	112′ x 15′
Pseudotsuga menziesii (tallest)	Douglas fir, British Columbia	152′ x 9′ 7½″
Pseudotsuga menziesii (stoutest)	Douglas fir, British Columbia	135′ x 13′ 10″
Sequoiadendron giganteum	Wellingtonia, California	145′ x 20′ 6″
Sequoia sempervirens	Californian redwood	121′ x 15′ 2″
Taxodium distichum	Swamp cypress, California	81′ x 6′
Thuja plicata	Western red cedar, British Columbia	115′ x 13′ 3″
	(Another specimen has a girth of 18 ft.—greatest recorded in Britain)	

Also in the arboretum stands a fine specimen of the Himalayan weeping spruce, *Picea smithiana*, while there is a good group of young Serbian spruce, *Picea omorika*, planted about 1942. These, and the specimen trees listed above, are all in the Lower Arboretum, but the visitors' attention is likely to be drawn, first of all, to the magnificent stands of Douglas fir on either side of the gravel road at the top of the hill.

A sample plot in the tall Douglas firs on the lower side of the road, measured in 1956, gave the following figures: Age of crop, 96 years; average height, 125 feet; average girth 8 ft. 5½ ins.; volume per acre, 9,742 hoppus feet, (=775 cubic metres per hectare). The stand on the upper side of the gravel road is noteworthy for the abundant growth of seedlings, mainly of Douglas fir but including other conifers, which have come up since a regeneration felling was made in 1940. This is an excellent illustration of the way in which foresters, through the process called natural regeneration, can secure the renewal of a stand of trees without the cost of replanting.

ORNAMENTAL DRIVE

Abies alba	European silver fir	135′ x 11′ 1″
Abies cephalonica	Greek fir	113′ x 6′ 11″
Abies grandis	Giant fir, Oregon	96′ x 3′ 8″
Abies nordmanniana	Nordmann fir, Caucasus (Tallest in England)	115′ x 6′ 11″
Abies pinsapo	Spanish fir (Tallest recorded in Britain)	102′ x 6′ 9″

Cedrus deodara	Deodar cedar, Himalayas	106′ x 5′ 7″
Chamaecyparis lawsoniana	Lawson cypress, British Columbia	112′ x 6′ 7″
Larix decidua	European larch, Switzerland	125′ x 6′ 10″
Picea abies	Norway spruce	110′ x 5′ 0″
Picea glauca	White spruce, Eastern North America	88′ x 5′ 11″
Picea mariana	Black spruce Eastern North America (Tallest recorded in Britain)	82′ x 5′ 2″
Picea rubra	Red spruce, Eastern North America (One of the tallest recorded)	88′ x 6′ 5″
Picea sitchensis	Sitka spruce, Alaska	135′ x 10′ 6″
Pinus nigra var. nigra	Austrian pine	94′ x 5′ 7″
Pinus nigra var. maritima	Corsican pine	106′ x 7′ 1″
Pinus strobus	Weymouth pine, Eastern United States	109′ x 9′ 8″
Pseudotsuga menziesii	Douglas fir, British Columbia	142′ x 14′ 6″
Sequoiadendron giganteum	Wellingtonia, California (Down a cross-ride to south, second tallest in Britain, and probably the tallest tree in the Forest)	156′ x 23′ 5″
Sequoia sempervirens	Californian redwood (Tallest in Britain)	132′ x 13′ 0″
Taxodium distichum	Swamp cypress, Florida	61′ x 5′ 4″
Thuja plicata	Western red cedar, British Columbia	122′ x 11′ 7″

Hauling out pine logs for a pulp mill

Measuring the length and girth of a felled oak log; branchwood will be used for fuel or charcoal

Seed sowing in the hardwood nursery at Lyndhurst

Selecting trees for thinning out from a Douglas fir plantation

SEEING THE TREES

I. THE ROUTE THROUGH BOLDERWOOD, MARK ASH, KNIGHTWOOD, AND THE ORNAMENTAL DRIVE TO BROCKENHURST

This is a good round tour of some fourteen miles to make by car or cycle from Lyndhurst or Brockenhurst. As a walk, it is rather long, though the bus service may be used between Brockenhurst and Lyndhurst. From Lyndhurst, take the Bournemouth road for $\frac{3}{4}$ mile; at Swan Green, take the right fork for Emery Down, and then, just past an inn, the first left turn. Proceed through the woods for three miles, gradually climbing the hill, until its summit is reached where the tall Douglas firs of Bolderwood are seen on the left. At the end of this enclosure fence, take a sharp left turn on to a gravel track across a strip of open forest, to the entrance to the Bolderwood Arboretum. Here another left turn leads one over a cattle grid and so into the woods, along a Forestry Commission road which is open to motorists.

This road passes the natural regeneration of Douglas fir in the Upper Arboretum, and the path down to the lower Arboretum may be seen on the right, opposite a cottage. Further on, the road runs downhill through Mark Ash wood. This includes some of the finest old beech in the Forest; small enclosures where experiments are being made in the regeneration of the woods when the old trees die and fall, may be noted on either side. The road then crosses another cattle grid into Knightwood Inclosure, and runs through more fine old beeches, and younger woods of Scots pine, Corsican pine, and Sitka spruce. A signpost shows the way to the famous Knightwood Oak, which lies to the left of the road. Just beyond that point, the route crosses the main road from Lyndhurst to Bournemouth, passing over two cattle grids. On the farther side, the route continues as a public road, which is tarred for most of the way. This is the well-known Ornamental Drive, flanked by rhododendrons and tall specimen trees, which have been labelled to aid their identification. Behind these lie flourishing plantations of oak and Douglas fir. Near Rhinefield Lodge, the road emerges on to the open forest, bears eastwards, and eventually leaves the woods of oak, Scots pine, and Douglas fir to cross a broad expanse of open heath. Here, making a contrast with the surrounding heather, there may be seen some of the improved pastures, with their lush green grass attracting many ponies. Further on, the road runs between fields to Brockenhurst village, best approached by taking the second left turn and crossing the watersplash. On proceeding ahead for half a mile, the main road from Lymington to Lyndhurst is struck close to Brockenhurst

Station. Thence a left turn leads back to Lyndhurst through some more attractive woodlands.

2. THE ROUTE TO PUCK PITS AND BOLDERWOOD ON FOOT

Puck Pits, one of the finest stands of mature conifers in the Forest, lies on the north side of Highlands Water Inclosure, about one mile from the nearest public road. The best way to find it is to make for the Stoney Cross cross-roads, which is served by buses from Southampton, Lyndhurst, and Ringwood. From this point, proceed south towards Lyndhurst for about 220 yards; then, opposite a large brick house, strike off to the right along a gravel track that runs towards a distant beech wood. Nearing the wood, this track bears right towards a gate near a pound for catching ponies, which will be seen on the left. Go through the gate, and bear half-left down a short steep grassy track towards the tall conifers. At the foot of this, a gravel track is reached, and by turning right on to this, one passes through the magnificent grove of European larches, Norway spruces, Douglas firs, and Corsican and Weymouth pines. A small enclosure where seedlings of these trees, and also those of oak and beech, have sprung up, may be seen on the left.

If it is desired to walk on to the Bolderwood Arboretum, two miles away, follow the track round until eventually a broad gravel road is encountered. Turn right on to this road, and follow it until it climbs the hill to emerge on the public highway. Then turn left, and strike off along the second gravel track on the right towards the tall Douglas firs of Bolderwood, which will be plainly seen ahead.

The return to Lyndhurst may be made by following the public road outside the Bolderwood fence in the downhill (easterly) direction; or else by following the gravel track (described in the previous section) through Bolderwood to Knightwood and the main Lyndhurst-Bournemouth road, where a left turn leads towards Lyndhurst.

ROUTES TO THE RUFUS STONE

The Rufus Stone, where according to tradition, King William II met his death while out hunting the deer, lies close to a by-road some two miles west of Cadnam. From Cadnam Roundabout follow the route signposted "Ringwood" to the top of the hill; there take a right-hand turn (signposted) down a steep hill, to find the stone on the left-hand side, near the hill foot (see page 9).

Alternatively, one may leave Cadnam by the route signposted "Fordingbridge and Salisbury". Follow this to the road junction beside the Bell Inn; then take a sharp left turn along a by-road.

This leads over a watersplash to the Sir Walter Tyrell Inn, and just beyond this the Rufus Stone will be seen on the right.

A pleasant round tour from Lyndhurst may be made by taking the second of these two routes, as far as the Stone, and then proceeding on up the hill to the Cadnam-Ringwood road. There turn left and shortly after right, and descend the hill into Minstead Village. There a right-hand turn leads over a watersplash and on to the road from Stoney Cross to Lyndhurst; turn left at that point, to reach Lyndhurst through Emery Down.

LAND AREAS

The total area of land within the New Forest Perambulation, under the New Forest Act of 1964, is 92,758 acres, or some 145 square miles. The map on the front endpaper shows the present boundary.

Of this area, 25,934 acres, or 40 square miles, is in private ownership. This figure includes 278 acres of tidal seashores along the Solent.

The remaining 67,024 acres, or 105 square miles, is held by the Crown, on the following terms:

	Acres
Forest Land	64,161
Crown Freehold	2,376
Crown Leasehold	487
TOTAL	67,024

In 1965, the Forest Land, parts of which may be enclosed from time to time for tree-growing under the terms of various Acts, was allocated as follows:

	Acres	*Acres*
Unenclosed woodlands	8,200	
Unenclosed commons and heaths ...	35,408	
Total of Unenclosed Forest Land ...		43,608
Enclosures under the 1877 Act, or prior legislation	17,646	
Ancient and Ornamental woods, enclosed for regeneration under the 1949 Act	897	
Verderers Enclosures, made under the 1949 Act	2,010	
Total of Enclosed Forest Land ...		20,553
TOTAL FOREST LAND ...		64,161

AREAS OF WOODLAND

The wooded areas of the New Forest, under Crown management, are today (1973) made up as follows:

	Acres
Enclosed woodlands on Forest Land	19,714
Enclosed woodlands on Crown freeholds	1,159
Enclosed woodlands on Crown leaseholds	487
Total of Enclosed Woodlands ...	21,360
Unenclosed woodlands on Forest Land	10,072
Total of all woodland, 1965 ...	31,432

There are thus some 31,400 acres, or 49 square miles, of Crown woodland within the New Forest Perambulation. Woods therefore comprise 47 per cent. of all land held by the Crown within the Forest.

HEIGHTS OF LAND

Elevations range from sea level to 414 feet on Long Cross Plain, north-east of Fritham. Much of the land forms broad plateaux, threaded by slow streams. Land to the south and east of Lyndhurst has a general level of 130 ft. Wilverley Plain in the south-west averages 200 ft. In the north-west, the broad heaths between Cadnam and Picket Post, traversed by the main A.31 highway towards Ringwood, stand 300 ft. above the sea. The highest ground, from 350 to 400 ft., neighbours the Cadnam-Fordingbridge road on the Forest's northern boundary. The general picture is one of a gradual slope from north-west down to south-east, giving broad views across the unseen Solent to the far hills on the Isle of Wight.

Woodcock

A NOTE ON BOOKS

THE most valuable modern scientific work is *The New Forest: An Ecological Study* by Colin R. Tubbs, published by David and Charles, Newton Abbot, in 1969, priced £2.50. Well illustrated, it embraces all aspects of field natural history and agricultural economy.

The classic work on the New Forest is that entitled *The New Forest, its History and Scenery*, by John R. Wise (Gibbings, London), first published in 1863. The main text deals with the history, topography, scenery, and customs of the Forest, whilst the appendices include lists of plants, birds and insects, and an interesting glossary of the local dialect. Although long out of print, it ran through several editions and second-hand copies are easily found.

There are many more recent works that describe and illustrate the Forest's attractions in a more popular style, including:

The New Forest	by G. E. Briscoe Eyre, 1883
The New Forest	by C. J. Cornish, 1894
The New Forest	by De Crespigny & Hutchinson, 1895
The New Forest	by Mrs. Rawnsley, 1904
The New Forest	by Horace Hutchinson, 1904
The New Forest	by E. Godfrey, 1912
Hampshire's Glorious Wilderness	by G. R. Tweedie, 1925
The New Forest Beautiful ...	by F. E. Stevens, 1925
Walking in the New Forest ...	by Joan Begbie, 1934

The New Forest ... ... by John C. Moore, 1934

The New Forest ... ... published by Messrs. Dent, 1960

Remarks on Forest Scenery (2 vols., 1791) is a well-known work by the Rev. William Gilpin, sometime Vicar of Boldre, who had much to say on the beauties of trees in the Forest landscape. An interesting record of sporting life in the Forest is to be found in *Thirty-five Years in the New Forest* (1915) by the Hon. Gerald Lascelles, a former Deputy Surveyor. The great authority on the Forest's archaeology was Heywood Sumner, whose published works include: *Ancient Earthworks of the New Forest*, 1917, *A Map of Ancient Sites in the New Forest*, 1923, *Guide to the New Forest*, 1924 (Reprinted by Dolphin Press, Christchurch, 1972, price £1.50) *Excavations in New Forest Roman Pottery Sites*, 1927, *Local Papers, Archaeological and Topographical, Hants, Dorset and Wilts*, 1931.

Dr. F. E. Kenchington has described the history and customs of the Commoners, and the war-time schemes for the improvement of the Forest grazing, very fully in *The Commoners New Forest* (Hutchinson, London, 1943). Very full accounts of the Forest's history and topography appear in the *Victoria County History of Hampshire* (1900, 6 vols.), which includes an informative article on forestry by Lascelles and Nisbet.

The best known work of fiction having a New Forest background is probably *The Children of the New Forest* (1853) by F. Maryatt, a story of Civil War days. R. D. Blackmore was the author of *Cradock Nowell; a Tale of the New Forest*, a three-volume work published in 1866. Mrs. Gaskell featured the New Forest in her *North and South*, 1855, as did Conan Doyle in his *The White Company*, 1891. Children of all ages will enjoy two more modern and well-illustrated stories by Allen W. Seaby, entitled *Skewbald, the New Forest Pony*, and *The White Hart*, the latter story being based on the life of a white deer which actually roamed the Rhinefield woods a few years ago.

A useful modern guide, giving details of some thirty walking routes, is *Russell's Graphic Guide to the New Forest*, published at 25p (postage 6p) by Russell & Co. (Southern Counties) Ltd., 54 Henstead Road, Southampton SO1 2DD. This firm also issues *Wild Life in the New Forest*, 20p, by Desmond Hawkins, with photos by Eric Ashby. Another up-to-date guide to the neighbourhood, entitled *The New Forest*, is published in Messrs. Ward, Lock & Co.'s series.

The Killing of William Rufus, by Duncan Grinnell-Milne (David & Charles, Newton Abbot, 1968, £1.75) is a thrilling investigation into the Forests' best-known historical event.

LOCALLY PRODUCED FORESTRY COMMISSION GUIDES

The following are available from: Forestry Commission, The Queen's House, High Street, Lyndhurst, Hants. SO4 7NH, or from local Information Centres and camp site shops. (Postage extra, 3p).

New Forest Guide Map, 20p.

Verderers Hall, Lyndhurst, 2p.

Bolderwood Woodland Walks, 4p.

Rhinefield Woodland Walks, 2½p.

BYELAWS

The *New Forest Byelaws* 1970 are published as Statutory Instrument 1970 No. 1068 by Her Majesty's Stationery Office, at 4p (6½p post free). The *New Forest Act* 1949 is also published by H.M.S.O., price 2½p (5p post free); also the *New Forest Act* 1964 at 5p (7½p post free); likewise the *New Forest Act* 1970 at 4p (6½p post free).

Guides to the Forest Parks and Areas of Public Access

Each guide includes articles on the surrounding forests, wild life, plant life, geology, history and tradition, walking and motoring routes, and camping facilities; and an indispensable map. Obtainable from the Government Bookshops listed on cover page iv, or through any bookseller.

ARGYLL FOREST PARK 35p (40½p)

BEDGEBURY, Kent (National Pinetum and Forest Plots) 90p (96½p)

CAMBRIAN FORESTS (Mid-Wales) (*Reprinting*)

DEAN FOREST AND WYE VALLEY FOREST PARK (*Reprinting*)

FORESTS OF NORTH-EAST SCOTLAND 25p (30½p)

GLAMORGAN FORESTS 25p (30½p)

GLEN MORE FOREST PARK (Cairngorms) 42½p (50p)

GLEN TROOL FOREST PARK (Galloway) (*Reprinting*)

NORTH YORKSHIRE FORESTS 65p (71½p)

FORESTS OF CENTRAL AND SOUTHERN SCOTLAND 62½p (73p)

FORESTRY IN THE WEALD 17½p (23p)

SNOWDONIA FOREST PARK 32½p (40p)

WESTONBIRT IN COLOUR 11p (13½p) (Westonbirt Arboretum, nr. Tetbury, Glos.)

KILMUN ARBORETUM AND FOREST PLOTS (near Dunoon, Argyll) 10p (12½p)

EAST ANGLIAN FORESTS 50p (56½p)

FOREST PARKS (Booklet 6) 20p (22½p)

Prices in brackets include postage.

A full list of Forestry Commission publications is available from the Forestry Commission, 25, Savile Row, London, W1X 2AY.

Printed in England for Her Majesty's Stationery Office by
Wells KPL Swindon Press, Swindon, Wilts.

Dd 505968 K 128 5/73

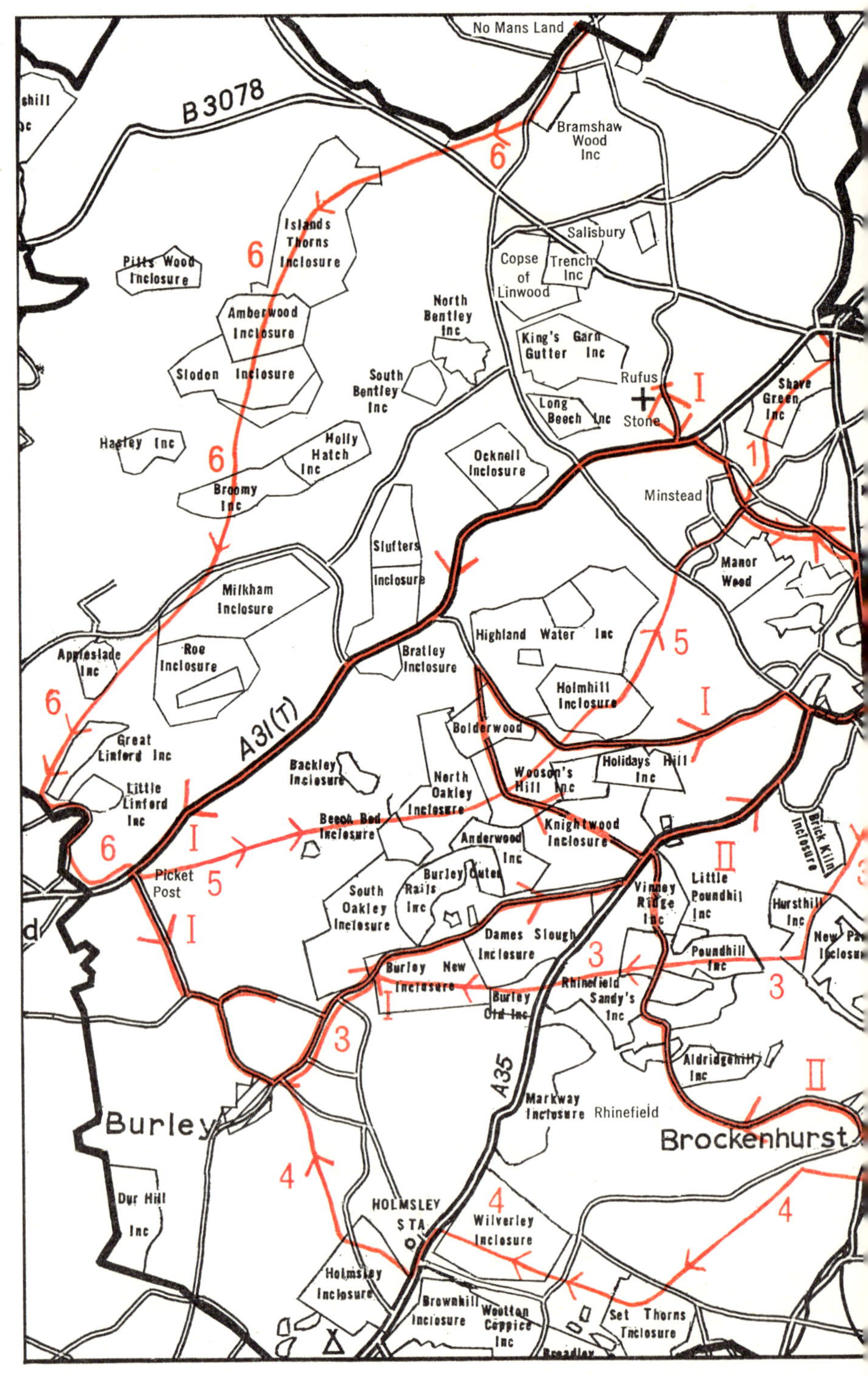

No Mans Land
B 3078
Bramshaw Wood Inc
Islands Thorns Inclosure
Pitts Wood Inclosure
Amberwood Inclosure
Slodon Inclosure
Salisbury
Copse of Linwood
Trench Inc
North Bentley Inc
South Bentley Inc
King's Garn Gutter Inc
Rufus Stone
Long Beech Inc
Shave Green Inc
Hasley Inc
Holly Hatch Inc
Broomy Inc
Ocknell Inclosure
Minstead
Slufters Inclosure
Milkham Inclosure
Manor Wood
Roe Inclosure
Appleslade Inc
Bratley Inclosure
Highland Water Inc
Holmhill Inclosure
Great Linford Inc
Little Linford Inc
A31(T)
Backley Inclosure
Bolderwood
North Oakley Inclosure
Wooson's Hill Inc
Holidays Hill Inc
Brick Kiln Inclosure
Beech Bed Inclosure
Anderwood Inc
Knightwood Inclosure
Picket Post
South Oakley Inclosure
Burley Rails Inc
Burley Outer
Vinney Ridge Inc
Little Poundhill Inc
Hursthill Inc
New Park Inclosure
Dames Slough Inclosure
Poundhill Inc
Burley New Inclosure
Burley Old Inc
Rhinefield Sandy's Inc
Aldridgehill Inc
A35
Markway Inclosure
Rhinefield
Burley
Brockenhurst
Dur Hill Inc
HOLMSLEY STA
Wilverley Inclosure
Holmsley Inclosure
Brownhill Inclosure
Wootton Coppice Inc
Set Thorns Inclosure
Broadley